CONFUCIAN WISDO

Confucian Wisdom for the 21st Century

A Selected Rendition

by

SHIU L. KONG

The Chinese University Press

Confucian Wisdom for the 21st Century:
A Selected Rendition
  Shiu L. Kong

© **The Chinese University of Hong Kong, 2009**

ISBN: 978–962–996–354–5

THE CHINESE UNIVERSITY PRESS
The Chinese University of Hong Kong
SHA TIN, N.T., HONG KONG
Fax: +852 2603 6692
    +852 2603 7355
E-mail: cup@cuhk.edu.hk
Web-site: www.chineseupress.com

Printed in Hong Kong

In loving memory of my mother who lived her 104-year
life characterized by Confucius wisdom,
while remaining illiterate

—∾∾—

To my children Lan, Ray, and Norm, and
my grandchildren Amelia, Rosalind, Averil, and Julian,
so that they may learn to appreciate their cultural wisdom

Contents

Preface

This is a new English presentation of Confucian wisdom as contained in the *Four Books* (*Si shu*), namely, the *Great Learning* (*Daxue*), *The Mean and Constancy* (*Zhongyong*), the *Analects* (*Lunyu*), and *Mencius* (*Mengzi*). For three thousand years such wisdom has been the guiding force for the Chinese as they transcended odds of ethnic diversity and social change to thrive in a continuous history, uninterrupted even when dynasties were ruled by people who were not mainstream Hans.

Today, we live in a global society marked by diversity and destruction. We are also threatened by uncertainty and environmental degeneration. As we move forward in the 21st century, we could do well to modify our way of life, by accepting our identity, adopting achievable goals, and sharing our happiness in harmony with people whose conditions and aspirations may not conform to our own.

Confucius was not a philosopher, for his thoughts and truths were not derived by logic. Rather, his wisdom reflected good common sense and insight inherited from his forefathers. His heritage was far and extensive. It included earthen and bronze utensils made ten thousand years before him, for cooking fine food, and praising imaginary gods. It also included elaborate descriptions of the universe, and man's place in it. The *Book of Changes* (*Yi jing*) regarded man as free and self-perfecting, capable of strengthening himself, and thriving in harmony with other living species on Earth.

Confucius was a disciplined and dedicated man. He was concerned with inculcating fine characters, nurturing wholesome families, and building a harmonious country among warring states. He did not succeed in all his goals. However, the concepts and principles of peace and human well-being that he had propounded had survived, valued by his countrymen even today. These concepts were narrated by his students in the *Four Books*, and enriched and expanded by scholars in ensuing centuries.

Education was the main theme of the Confucian books. They were, however, not effective texts for learning. Written in classical Chinese, even simple ideas may obscure understanding, hidden in the economy of words and, at the same time, the multiple meanings in the same word when applied to different situations often caused confusion. For example, the word *ren*, with the usual English translation of *benevolence*, carried the meanings of love, kindness, sympathy, warmth, tolerance, respect, caring, openness, altruism, etc. As recorded in the books, Confucian used some fifty practical applications in life situations to illustrate these meanings to his students. A second example is the word *junzi* (gentleman). It meant persons as they were and as they should be, prudent, inquisitive, enterprising, kind, polite, just, virtuous, aspiring, and responsible.

Yet, Confucian ideas are easy to understand, as well as readily applicable. They have been effectively transmitted orally from generation to generation to become an integral part of Chinese life. Today, one could easily encounter in a nearby playground a child trying to deter a bully by saying: "Hey, do not do to others what you would not wish them to do to you," and the latter would abort his *unrenly* act, muttering, "You would not have it so easy next time."

In my own experience, I have always remembered and acted on the Confucian saying that my illiterate mother had taught me early in life: "Help other people to establish themselves whenever you wish to establish yourself; enable others to express themselves and communicate whenever you wish to accomplish the same." I do not know how my mother could have understood the profound meaning and utility of many such sayings in her repository. I do know, however, that she lived her 104-year-old life happily, in three eventful dynasties and in Canada, overcoming renewing challenges.

The two sayings mentioned above encapsulate the essence of the Confucian wisdom. The first pertains to an awareness of self in relationship to fellow human beings, showing respect. The second describes the quality of good character relative to responsibility and love toward others, enshrining harmony.

I only managed to read the *Four Books* and their commentaries thoroughly after I retired from forty years of teaching in universities in many countries and cultures. I realized that, while these books were basically about education and living meaningful and wholesome lives, they had been treated as books of philosophy and ethics, reserved for scholarly attention. They have also been abused by self-serving activists to achieve political ends. They must now be returned to the common people for appreciation and application.

In this vein, I have attempted to interpret and translate these books in tune with psycho-educational principles and methods. I have left out chapters and sections of the original writing in order to put important concepts in sharp focus. These include discussions on politics and governance, and repetitious narrations on legends and ancient events. I have also used positive statements to avoid any confusion caused by negative expressions. In their present form, these Confucian books should be inviting and understandable to a wider range of readers.

Hundreds of Confucian Institutes have sprung up in universities and cultural organizations across China and around the globe in recent years. There appears to be a new awareness of the timeless value of Confucian ideas and way of life. Perhaps this is because we are finding ourselves drifting down a stream of techno-economic changes that neither our senses nor our psyche can freely cope. Even children are experiencing stress as they grow up today.

We need to re-tune our focus and directions. Human beings need to be their own masters in order to be free and creative. Human happiness can only be found in serene and nurturing environments, where people live in harmony with one another, and with Mother Nature. I hope my readers will find in this publication not only ideas and behavioral guidelines, but also a new orientation to life.

My late friend Lee Hon Wing had read the draft manuscript and offered valuable suggestions. He was an exemplary teacher and a *junzi*. I miss him. May his legacy imbedded in this book inspire readers of every age, gender, and culture.

Shiu L. Kong
Toronto

A portrait of Confucius by Tang artist Wu Daozi (680–740).

The Apricot Platform in the courtyard of the Confucius Temple in Qufu, Shandong province.

The tomb of Confucius in Qufu, Shandong province. The inscription reads "Tomb of the Prince of Literary Excellence and Sagely Achievements" (Dacheng Zhixing Wenxuanwang).

Education is of primary importance in Confucian tradition, and teachers are respected and worshiped along with gods and parents. Shown here is a tablet as a symbol for worship in the living room of most middle-class homes of bygone days. The five words on the tablet read as heaven, earth, emperor, parents, and teacher. Today, similar tablets might still appear in a few homes in Taiwan or Singapore.

Technology and art were at a high during Confucius' time, as attested by this army of ten thousand terracotta soldiers, horses, and carriages unearthed from the tomb of Qin Shihuang, the first emperor of a united China. Close examination revealed that every single soldier had a unique character, identifiably different from his comrades.

The author is shown here with the relief statue of Damo, the first Indian monk who brought Buddhism into China. It quickly became fused with Confucian wisdom to develop into a new way of spiritualism and lifestyle called Chan (Zen). Today, the belief system called Confucianism is a fusion of Daoist thought, Confucian thought, and Buddhist thought. In it the highest achievement of human beings is inward peace and outward harmony.

A typical study of a Confucian scholar. In its simplicity is seen a rich display of art objects and a well-tended plant. Together they conjure a serenity conducive to the pursuit of scholarly activities.

A typical ancestor hall in rural China maintained even today. Confucianism emphasizes ancestor worship as a binding force for the family, as well as the perpetuation of continuity of a clan or people. Lanterns are hung each time a male child is born into the clan. The four characters on the plaque read from right to left "forebears' achievements, clannish virtue."

In Confucian thought the family is the pivotal anchor for the individual, and the building block of society. For centuries up until recently clannish living was the norm in the middle and upper classes. Shown here is the central section of a round house for clannish life, with the ancestor hall given prominence in the center.

A painting of Mencius, who is generally regarded as the most famous Confucian after Confucius himself. His interpretation of Confucianism has been considered the ortho-dox version by subsequent Chinese philosophers, especially the Neo-Confucians of the Song dynasty.

A one-on-one tutorial at a typical Confucian school in ancient times. The teacher marks out passages in the books to be studied and tests the students on their meanings a few days later. It is up to the students to figure out and tell the class what meanings they derive from the text.

In the days of public examination held at the county and national levels, villages whose sons achieved high standards are granted flag poles to mark their scholarly success. The poles are elaborately carved individually and not necessarily used to fly flags. Competition among villages is fierce. Those who are successful are visible from far away.

In ancient China, a system of public examinations was developed based on Confucian wisdom. Japan and Korea also adopted this system and the concept became universal in modern times. Shown here, in well-kept condition, is a row of ancient examination booths in the side yard of a famous temple near Nagasaki, Japan. Each booth was occupied by a single candidate. The booth was tightly enclosed so that no communication with others was possible, Even ventilation was to be desired.

Today, visitors believe that if they tie written wishes for academic success to the door frame they would do well in school. Or, like the visitor shown, one may make a wish by holding the colorful rope and expect the wish to come true.

A short distance from the examination booths, flanked by the author, stands a finely constructed *bi zhong*, Tomb of Ink Brushes. Buried in it were the used brushes of all successful scholars. In time, other people buried their used brushes here with the belief that they would be blessed by their accomplished forerunners. Today, students come to worship the tomb before their exams, hoping to do well.

The Great Learning

Introduction

The *Great Learning* is originally a section of *Li ji* (*Book of Rites*), the work of Confucian scholars of the Qin and Han dynasties. The Song dynasty scholar Zhu Xi edited it into an independent book. He also made elaborate annotations to show the authentic meanings of the original text, as well as to add meaning to them.

Since then, the new text has become a basic textbook for Confucian education, together with *The Mean and Constancy*, the *Analects*, and *Mencius*. Named the *Four Books,* these texts have been regarded as the essence of Confucian wisdom, or classics of Chinese thought.

There are two basic parts. They are Confucius' Teaching and Commentaries of Zeng Zi, one of Confucius' prominent students. The first part deals with methods of learning, self-cultivation, and leadership. The second part discusses methods of investigation and self-actualization as they pertain to excellence and perfection. In both cases, much is said about human nature, potentials for achieving goodness and perfection, social skills, and human ideals.

Confucius offered no profound views or effective methods on governance. For him, good governance would emerge through the proper education of the individual, especially the gentleman, who would build good families and therefore a good society.

Embedded in these views and expectations are the principles of ethics and education based on the psychology of man and his way of life, culminating in peace and harmony.

SLK

Part One: Confucius' Teaching

The essence of the *Great Learning* (Learning of the Gentleman) is:

- to enable the learner to know his inherent virtues so that he is not driven by selfish desires,
- to inspire fellow human beings so that everyone will love to learn,
- to pursue one's studies until one has reached the acme of perfection and then to consolidate the acquired knowledge.

Consolidation of one's knowledge facilitates the setting of goals and mental stability. A stable mind forms the basis of satisfaction and tranquility, which alert awareness and deliberation, leading to perfection.

All matters and human affairs have beginnings and ends. Knowing the sequences and priorities of development is akin to knowing the subject matter of the *Great Learning*, the *Way*.

Ancient students committed to studying the *Great Learning* were inspired to lead and to become rulers of state. They approached their studies by following these sequential attainments:

- in order to rule a state one must first regulate one's family;
- to regulate the family one must cultivate a perfect character;
- to cultivate good character one must purify one's mind;
- to purify the mind one must be sincere with one's wishes, modifying them with knowledge which grew out of investigations of matters and human affairs.

Reasoning in reverse order:

- investigation leads to knowing,
- knowing leads to sincere wishes,
- sincere wishes lead to the cultivation of the mind, which facilitates the formation of good character.

Therefore, as it applied equally to the emperor and the common citizen, the cultivation of a person's character is the foundation of all forms of achievement.

On recognition that the family is the important building block of society, a gentleman must first pay great attention to regulating his family before he aspires to the distant goal of ruling his state.

Part Two: Zeng Zi's Commentaries

On the bathtub of Emperor Tang were inscribed these words: If you can one day do a self-renewal, do it every day, and repeat doing so ceaselessly.

The Kang Pronouncement said that a good leader should encourage his people to habitually renew themselves. The *Book of Poetry (Shi jing)* said: "Although Zhou is an ancient state, it was renewed by the ordinance of Emperor Wen."

Therefore, a great leader makes the most effort to encourage his people to make frequent renewals. (2)

Confucius said: "On hearing litigation cases, I am like any other person. However, I believe in elimination of the need for litigation from its roots. It can be achieved when those people who are devoid of moral principles are not allowed to flatter, and everyone in the state is taught to delineate what is right and what is wrong. This is called understanding the basics, the ultimate perfection in learning."

[Commentaries by Zhu Zi]

Investigations are done by man, the knower. He will examine, observe, and test all things encountered to find out how they work....

All things bound by Heaven and Earth function in their own ways. Because these ways vary without limits, no learning can be complete and perfect.

The purpose of the *Great Learning* is to explain and teach the principles and methods that govern things, and to impress upon the learner that it is important to proceed from what he knows to what he does not know, and to do so until the utter limits of investigating and knowing are reached.

The student will, after long studies and critical investigations, experience a sudden understanding which will enable him to comprehend the totality of everything, the appearance and inner essence, the coarse and subtle truths. At that point, he will realize that his mind is naturally intelligent and related to all the things learned.

This is called investigation. It is also called learning to know, the most effective way of knowing. (5)

Being sincere in thought and wishes means avoiding self-deception.

Sincerity is intuitive. Just as one naturally detests a bad smell or loves a beautiful color, one can also intuitively experience the good feeling of sincerity and the evil feeling of deception. A gentleman should be sensitive to how he feels even when he is alone.

A base man is prone to deceive his fellow man. He would hide his actions behind a gentleman's good deeds so as to pretend that he is also virtuous. He would also foolishly believe that people do not see his evil actions and disguises.

Sincerity dwells in a man's heart and manifests in his actions. The gentleman watches how he feels even when he is alone.

Zeng Zi said: "One must be critically aware of the watching of ten eyes and the pointing of ten fingers in one's daily life.

"A rich man decorates his house to feel proud. On the other hand, a virtuous man cultivates himself to achieve tranquility of mind and relaxation of body. A gentleman naturally chooses to be sincere so his mind and body are in their healthy and happy state." (6)

The correct way to cultivate good character is to set one's mind in a right position, sensitive and objective.

When a man is angry, his mind is not right.

When he is desirous of something, his mind is not right.

When he is in distress or sorrow, his mind is not right.

When he is absent-minded, he will not see as he looks, not hear as he listens, and not taste as he eats.

This is why we need to set our minds right. (7)

A man who sets out to regulate his family must first cultivate his own character.

People are generally biased or partial in the way they conduct themselves.

A man tends to like another person who is closely related to him, and to dislike a person whom he despises.

He will respect and stand in awe as he encounters things and people that he reveres.

He sympathizes with people in sorrow, and detests those behaviors that are impolite and inconsiderate.

In the space between Heaven and Earth, perhaps only a very few people can behave in such ways as to recognize the shortcomings of those they love, or to accept the good qualities of those they hate.

A wise saying denotes: "A loving father is blind to see his son's wicked behavior, just as he is never satisfied with the thriving stalks growing in his field."

Thus, a man will not be able to regulate his family before he has successfully cultivated a good character in himself. (8)

The Mean and Constancy

風俗通義過譽第四

孔子稱大哉中庸之為德其至矣乎又曰君子之道忠恕而已矣至於
之所必討蓋觀過知仁謂中心篤誠而無妨於化者故責其違理曰
過譽也

長沙太守汝南到懼君童少時為郡功曹郡俗冬饗百里內
縣皆齎牛酒到府宴飲時太守司徒歐陽歙臨饗禮訖教曰
西部督郵繇延天資忠貞奉性公方典部折衝摧破姦雄不
嚴而治嚴錄功顯之于朝主薄讀教以教而不能者勤
今與諸儒共論延資性邪佞外方內圓朋黨構姦罔上害民所在荒
覆權按延貪鯢以君主懷子天明府有言延愛睍懂
前跪曰正橾鯢以君告謝子天明府有言延愛睍懂
亂處而不治怒歷並作百姓苦之而明府以惡為善毀肱莫

Introduction

The Song scholar Zhu Xi, deriving from his teachers the Chengs, said: "Not being inclined to the extremes of ideas and things is called *zhong*, the mean; not being subject to change is called *yong*, constancy."

Zhong is the correct course in the universe; *yong* constitutes the basic principles in that course.

This book, *The Mean and Constancy*, describes human psychology, as taught in the Confucian school. The basic content was taken from *Li ji*, and compiled by the grandson of Confucius, Zi Si, for the benefit of Mencius, the renowned Confucian scholar.

In its present form, *The Mean and Constancy* is a component part of the Confucian classics the *Four Books*, the basic textbook in traditional Chinese education for over two millennia. It is the most authoritative text on psychology that has influenced the way the Chinese understand human nature, human purpose, human relationship, human learning, and human aspiration. What is construed in concepts such as the "Chinese way of life," "Chinese philosophy," or "Chinese mentality" etc. is intricately reflected in the narrations in this book. However, and somewhat unfortunately, I have not come across any rendition which uses the word psychology to refer to its contents. Instead, the narrower terms of "nature of the mind," "functions of the mind," and "communication of the mind" etc. were used. I believe that casting the many useful concepts and beliefs in the context of psychology would help us better appreciate the wisdom of Confucius in the 21st century.

Contrary to the conventional translation of the book title as the *Doctrine of the Mean*, I believe it is more true and comprehensive to use the title *The Mean and Constancy*. The reader will agree with me as soon as they read the Preface of the book. More importantly, there are no doctrines in the book. There are theories and advice. Ancient doctrines are usually pedantic. On the other hand, theories and advice remain vibrant over time, awaiting new tests and applications.

SLK

Preface

Chen Zi said: "Not being inclined to the extremes of ideas and things is called *zhong*, not being subject to change is called *yong*."

The *zhong* is the correct course in the universe, while the *yong* constitutes the basic principles along that course. This book describes human nature and psychology as discussed by Confucius and his students. The given theories and advice all originated from a single belief. As applied to ten thousand situations, these theories and advice worked effectively to revert to the same belief.

This belief can fill the universe when it is unfolded. It will recede to mystery when it is rolled up. In either case, it has resulted from solid studies, and its intricacy knows no bounds.

Thus, as our readers learn something from this belief in their reading and explorations, they will be intrigued by its practical value, as applications are made repeatedly throughout their lives.

"A man's nature is determined by his natural endowments. He develops his way of life when he functions in concert with his nature. And the process by means of which he builds his character is his education.

"A man's way of life is always with him. If detached, it is not his way. That is why a gentleman guards his behavior even when no one is watching, and he is cautious even when no criticism is heard.

"Nothing is more visible than when it is hidden. Nothing is more evident than when it is reduced to the simplest form. That is why a gentleman is especially careful in his behavior when he is alone.

"When delight, anger, sorrow, and satisfaction are not yet

expressed, the mind is in equilibrium. It is called *zhong*, the mind in a state of the *mean*.

"When these emotions are expressed, and moderated by moral principles, harmony ensues.

"*Zhong*, or equilibrium, is a fundamental state of mind for everyone.

"Harmony is a state of mind in which people communicate effectively, sharing the same moral principles.

"When both equilibrium and harmony are achieved, all things in the universe will be in their ordered positions, and people can develop and thrive." (1)

Confucius said: "A gentleman acts according to principles of the *The Mean and Constancy*. A base man acts counter to them.

"A gentleman embodies the *The Mean and Constancy* because it is his belief. He gages all his behaviors with its inherent principles.

"On the other hand, a base man nullifies *The Mean and Constancy* because he has no respect for what is right and proper." (2)

Confucius said: "Perfect is the belief of *The Mean and Constancy*. What a pity that so few people are making good use of it now." (3)

Confucius said: "I know why the way of *The Mean and Constancy* has not been followed enough. Those who know it well have taken it as a belief for admiration rather than for practice, while those who do not understand have no basis for practice.

"I know why the belief of *The Mean and Constancy* is not

generally understood. Those who are able and intelligent practice it at random, while those who are not up to it simply ignore it.

"Everybody eats and drinks. I wonder if there are not people who do so without knowing the taste." (4)

Confucius said: "What a discerning knower Emperor Shun was! He loved to observe and inquire. He concealed the shortcomings in other people but revealed what was good in them. He took in the extreme views of his people and delineated *The Mean and Constancy* for reference in shaping his policies. Such was Shun The Great Emperor." (6)

Confucius said: "People boast of being clever, even when they do not know how to escape from a trap laid especially for them.

"People believe that they know it all. However, even when they have decided to practice the way of *The Mean and Constancy*, they fail to continue to do so for a month." (7)

Confucius said: "This is how Hui was. He had willed himself to follow the belief of *The Mean and Constancy* and, whenever he got a good result, he would hold the experience close to his heart so that he would not lose it." (8)

Student Lu asked about fortitude in character.

Confucius asked him to phrase his question more precisely, for the fortitude of northerners is different from that of

southerners, or whether he wanted to know how he could cultivate fortitude for himself.

The Master then went on to explain: "Our southerners
demonstrate their fortitude by teaching people with forbearance
and caring, accommodating those who behaved badly. Our
northerners show their fortitude by revering success and
principles. They sleep with weapons tugged to their side, fearing
no death.

"A gentleman of true fortitude relates to people in harmony
while holding fast to his belief in *The Mean and Constancy*.

"A man of true fortitude stands firm in a neutral, unbiased
position.

"A man of true fortitude maintains his way of life when his
country is secure and prosperous; he does not waver in the face
of chaos and misery." (10)

Confucius said: "I would not seek fame in history by advocating
heretical theories, or being engaged in weird behaviors. A gentleman should follow the way of *The Mean and Constancy*, and
will not stop half-way through, even when others do.

"A gentleman stays in the way of *The Mean and Constancy*
all his life, regretting not for a moment if it would lead to
personal obscurity. I dare say, perhaps only a sage can do this
completely." (11)

"The way of *The Mean and Constancy*, as practiced by the
gentleman, is laborious and not easily seen.

"This is so well known that even ordinary couples would
talk about it in their daily chatters, or practice it in daily
routines. As for its highest wisdom, not even sages would understand all the details.

"However vast and rich our universe may be, some people

may still find dissatisfaction with what it contains. When the gentleman speaks of the profound truth in the way of *The Mean and Constancy*, not even our universe is big enough to house it. When he speaks of the nuances, it is natural that not everyone in the universe can understand.

"It is said in the *Book of Poetry*, 'Raise your head high, you will see hawks soaring in the sky. Drop your head low, you will see fishes in the deep.' It tells of how the gentleman searched high and low to find the *Way*.

"The simple elements of the way of *The Mean and Constancy* can be easily seen from the daily interactions between husbands and wives. Once you have understood the basic principles of the *Way*, you will see the harmonious relationships among all people and things bound by Heaven and Earth." (12)

Confucius said: "The way of *The Mean and Constancy* is not remote from man.

"There are people who think that, because the *Way* is close by, it is not worth much. They therefore seek what is grand and difficult to reach, believing it to be better. But that is not the *Way*.

"It is said in the *Book of Poetry*: 'When carving the handle of an axe, the prototype is in your hand....'

"Hence a gentleman teaches others just as he teaches himself, completing the process the moment the learner knows how to correct his faults.

"A man able to practice loyalty and forbearance is not distant from the way of *The Mean and Constancy*. So, do not do to others what you would not wish them to do to you.

"The *Way* of the gentleman has four dimensions, not one of which is attained by me. What respect and service I ask of my son, I am not able to deliver to my father.

"What I ask of my subordinates, I cannot yet deliver to my king. What respect I ask from my younger brother, I fall short of paying the same to my elder brother. What treatment I ask of my friends, I cannot do the same to them.

"Although I have been careful with my words and acts so that they do not deviate from the *Way*, I must say that I have not been successful. I should remind myself of this fact, and I should never attempt to overestimate my ability.

"A man should think of his relative behavior as he speaks. He should also be mindful of what he has said as he acts. A gentleman should follow the same principle to remain a gentleman." (13)

"A gentleman adapts positively to his position and situation, seeking not to exceed the limits.

"He enjoys abundance when he is rich. He adapts to material scarcity when he is destitute. He adopts the local customs when he lives among barbarians. He copes with sorrow and crisis when he is bothered by loss and distress.

"A gentleman remains tranquil and contented regardless of who he is with. He will not abuse his subordinates. Nor would he flatter his superiors.

"If a man cultivates himself to behave according to the *Way*, and not be a liability to society, then nobody would complain about him.

"Hence, a gentleman can ride on change as the realities of life require. He will be happy to accept how things are without any murmur against the gods or his own kind.

"In contrast, a base man will seek luck by risking danger."

Confucius said: "A gentleman acts much like engaging in a game of archery. Whenever he misses the bull's eye, he reflects on his aim, seeking to correct it so that he can do better the next round." (14)

A gentleman follows the way of *The Mean and Constancy* like embarking on a long voyage. He starts from where he stands. He tests the low grounds before he climbs a mountain peak.

It is said in the *Book of Poetry*: "A happy marriage is akin to the melodic interplay of the harp and the lute. A synergic relationship among family siblings is akin to musical harmony that lingers in the air. May you enjoy your family life, and allow everyone in your home to thrive."

Confucius said: "Given such happiness in the family, any parent would feel fulfilled." (15)

Confucius said: "The blessing of the gods and spirits is rich and pervasive. Though they cannot be seen or heard, their powers are felt with all the things they have created for us.

"Let everybody fast, bathe, and put on their formal dresses to respect them in traditional rites. Let us worship them in their omnipresence, from above permeating Heaven, and around us left and right.

"It is said in the *Book of Poetry*: 'The advent of the gods is not announced, nor can it be surmised. But can you be indifferent in receiving it?'

"True sincerity dwells in people's heart. However invisible it might be, it is radiating and not repressible." (16)

Confucius said: "What is filial piety? It is the inheritance and continuation of the goals of our forefathers, and the recording and dissemination of past events....

"We pay our respects to our ancestors with music and the rites, and show our affection to those they loved.

"We serve the deceased as if they were alive, and respect the departed as if they were still in our presence.

"That is filial piety in its ultimate sense." (19)

Confucius said: "*Ren*, the spirit of benevolence, is to love people, with the priority of loving one's parents.

"*Yi*, the spirit of righteousness, is to do what is right, and to show deference to those who are able and kind....

"There are five universal duties and obligations. They are to be carried out within the bounds of three virtues.

"The five duties exist between sovereign and ministers, father and son, husband and wife, elder and younger brothers, and a person and his friends.

"The three virtues are wisdom, benevolence, and courage, to be combined into a single force of action.

"Some people are born to know. Others know through learning. Still others know out of solving practical problems. However, the wisdom they seek is one and the same.

"As for practicing what is good and virtuous, some people do it naturally, others do it for gain; still others do it as a reluctant obligation. However, the effect is the same regardless of how the act is conducted."

Confucius said: "To love to learn is wise, to vigorously fulfill one's obligations is close to being benevolent, and to be aware of shame is like being courageous. He who understands how these three forces work will know how to cultivate a good and virtuous character. He who possesses a good and virtuous character is fit to lead others. By extension, such a man will succeed in achieving peace among nations.

"Sincerity is the way of Heaven. But, it is natural that man bears sincerity in his words and actions....

"He who is sincere is bent on learning extensively, inquiring critically, contemplating meticulously, judging impartially, and practicing sincerity earnestly.

"A sincere man may not be wise. But, once he engages in learning, he will not stop until he understands thoroughly. He may not know how to think. But, once he engages in thinking, he will not retire until his problems are solved. He may not be used to acting. But, once he begins to take action, he will not rest until the job is done.

"Such a man will spare no effort in achieving his goal. If another person succeeds in one operation, he is ready to do one hundred. If yet another person succeeds with ten operations, he will do one thousand.

"Such a man may be dull, but he will become intelligent. He may be weak, but he will become strong." (20)

"He who knows the virtues sincerely is a natural knower.

"He who becomes sincere through learning has benefited by education.

"Sincerity enables a person to understand and know.

"Understanding and knowledge help a person to be sincere." (21)

"Being sincere is a self-fulfilling act. The sincere way is a self-directed way.

"Sincerity embraces the beginning and end of all things; nothing is of any significance without it.

"Therefore, a gentleman reveres sincerity with utmost care.

"Being sincere is not limited to achieving success for oneself, but also extends to achieve success for everyone and everything.

"To achieve self-success is a mark of benevolence. To facilitate the success of all people is a mark of wisdom and compassion. Both acts are natural virtues shared by all human beings. They combine to function effectively in all places at all times." (25)

"A gentleman conducts himself in a way that is unobtrusive, step by step.... His actions and speeches are plain and inspiring, gentle and insistent. He knows what is feasible in a grand design, where the wind blows, what is hidden behind the obvious, and hence the path to success in achieving virtue....

"A gentleman has no regrets when he reflects on his past, nor is he ashamed of his deeds....

"A gentleman gains the respect of other people while remaining tranquil, and he earns the trust of others without having to say much....

"A gentleman does not need to use reward to motivate his people to strive for excellence, nor does he need to throw a temper to induce fear....

"As a gentleman maintains his proven wisdom and projects his well-earned dignity, peace and prosperity will prevail in his domain...."

Confucius concluded: "It is frivolous and ineffective to transform people with the use of one's command or authority." (33)

The Analects

天地間至尊者道至貴者德而已矣至難得者人

別子通書

師友上第二十四

師友下第二十五

能化而齊故顏子亞聖朱熹曰至尊可二字之觀

者見其大而忘其小焉爾見其大則心泰心泰則

無不足無不足則富貴貧賤處之一也處之一則

者獨何心哉夫富貴人所愛也顏子不愛不求而樂乎貧

其樂夫富貴人所愛也在陋巷人不堪其憂而不改

顏子一簞食一瓢飲

顏子第二十三

為一實萬分萬一各正小大有定

矣二氣五行化生萬物五殊二實二本則一是萬

理性命第二十二

厥彰厥微匪靈弗瑩剛善剛惡柔亦如之中焉止

公於己者公於人未有不公於己而能公於人也

公明第二十一

明不至則疑生明無疑也謂能裝為明可帝千里

軍直則公公則溥明通公溥庶矣乎

Introduction

This book is a record of the teaching and deeds of Confucius and his students. Two main themes constitute the fabrics which form the discourses that reverberate throughout the whole book, namely, how education facilitates intellectual and moral development, and how self-awareness and self-restraint enhance interpersonal relations, the building blocks of peace and harmony in communities and states.

As a narrative of teaching-learning processes, this book provides vivid accounts of Confucius' teaching method, as well as his treatment of individual differences in ability and aspiration among his students. Some educators regard this book as a presentation of Confucian pedagogy.

Here, one finds detailed expositions of the concepts of benevolence and righteousness, as well as those of the four cardinal principles of Chinese morality, *li* (propriety), *yi* (righteousness), *lian* (frugality), *chi* (sense of shame). Poetry is emphasized for appreciation of the richness of the Chinese language, and for reinforcing a sense of history as reflected in ancient legends and heroes.

Like all good teachers, Confucius encouraged his students to learn by asking questions. But he seldom gave direct answers. Instead, he provided situations and examples to provoke thought and self-rectification. However, he was not without faults as a teacher, because he overtly displayed favoritism among his students.

There is a dearth of information on the kind of school and classroom environments in which Confucius and his students lived and learned. His students were all males and mostly adults.

They traveled and learned together quite often. And he allowed some of his advanced students to teach the novices. He and his students also openly shared their feelings and affections. For all this broad coverage of life and education, morality and social order, this book is given its unique title, *The Analects*.

SLK

Confucius said: "How delightful it is to learn and practice one's knowledge and skills consistently. How pleasurable it is to have friends visiting from afar.

"A gentleman is not concerned that other people may not notice his scholarship; he commits himself to studies because of their intrinsic value." (1.1)

Student You said: "People who respect and care for their elders and superiors seldom offend them.

"There have been no cases in which people who do not easily offend their elders are keen to disrupt social order.

"A gentleman knows himself. He anchors his behaviors on moral principles grounded in his culture. Filial piety and fraternal love are rooted in the principle of benevolence, *ren*." (1.2)

Confucius said: "People who speak skillful words and display submissive manners are not benevolent." (1.3)

Student Zeng said: "I reflect three times a day, asking:

"Have I been truthful and done my best to the people I serve?

"Have I been honest and sincere in dealing with my friends?

"Have I learned and applied my teacher's teaching?" (1.4)

Confucius said: "At home, children and youth should love and serve their parents.

"They should respect their elders in the community.

"They should speak with deliberation and commitment,

love people without prejudice, and keep company with those who are good and benevolent.

"In addition, they should study the arts and letters." (1.6)

Student Xia said: "A man who loves his wife for her virtue more than her beauty, who serves and supports his parents with utmost respect, who is ready to sacrifice his life for his country, and who is trustworthy as he interacts with his friends, should be regarded as a cultured man, even if he has not benefited from schooling." (1.7)

Confucius said: "A gentleman who is frivolous will not command respect, and his learning would not be solid.

"A gentleman guards his loyalty and sincerity vehemently; he does not make friends with people whose ability and moral standards are inferior to his.

"Whenever he makes a mistake he would correct it steadfastly." (1.8)

Student Zeng said: "Take great care in performing the funeral rites to your parents, and persist in paying respect to your distant ancestors. You will establish a firm moral foundation in your community." (1.9)

Confucius said: "Take note of a person's aspirations when he is under his father's wings, and watch his behaviors when he is on his own after his father has passed away. You will know he is filial if he follows his father's path for three years without change." (1.11)

Student You said: "Harmony is the central consideration when practicing the rules of *li*, propriety. That was what our ancient sage kings emphasized as they ruled.

"However, when it is necessary to relax aspects of these principles under special circumstances, insist on forging harmonious relations with people. There is no need to impose the principles of propriety on everyone." (1.12)

Student You said: "Agreement is similar to *yi*, righteousness. A contract that is drawn on the principles of *yi* holds both parties accountable.

"Respect is similar to *li*, propriety. Use it whenever you encounter people of virtue, then you will not shame your parents. You will also surely earn their affection." (1.13)

Confucius said: "A gentleman seeks not satisfaction in good food, nor comfort in fine dwelling. Instead, he is committed to studying earnestly and to expressing his ideas with carefully chosen words.

"He is also alert in seeking the advice of people of ability and virtue." (1.14)

Student Gong asked Confucius: "How should we appraise a poor man who does not exercise flattery, or a rich man who does not display conceit?"

Confucius replied: "Good. But I prefer a poor man who is contented, and a rich man who practices *li*, propriety."

Gong murmured: "Every time I asked you a question, your response would inspire me to understand something beyond my existing comprehension. It reminds me of a verse in the *Book of Poetry*, saying, 'To learn is like perfecting a jade stone, repeatedly cutting and filing, carving and polishing.'"

The Master then said: "Now I can show you the beauty and power of our poetry tradition. You will discover from it our past achievement and know how to chart your future plans." (1.15)

Confucius said: "Do not be perturbed that many people do not know you well. Be alarmed that you do not know other people as well as you should." (1.16)

Confucius said: "The 300 poems in the *Book of Poetry* contain a single message, namely, keep a pure mind and harbor no evil thoughts." (2.2)

Confucius said: "Lead people with virtue and just laws. If you regulate people with the use of standard punishment, they will resort to mere avoidance, and feel no shame.

"If you lead people by helping them to know virtue, they will know shame, and regulate their own behavior." (2.3)

Confucius said: "I had my mind set on formal studies when I was fifteen.

"At thirty, I established my goals and approaches in knowledge as in life.

"At forty, I had a good understanding of things and people, free of doubts.

"At fifty, I knowingly accepted the givens of life.

"At sixty, I detected truth readily, accepting them as they emerge.

"At seventy, I felt free to do as I pleased, being mindful only not to overstep traditional rules." (2.4)

Student Meng asked about filial piety, whereupon Confucius replied: "Do not counter the principles of virtue."

As another student Fan was on duty pushing Confucius' cart, the teacher recounted the previous conversation for his benefit. But Fan did not understand.

Confucius then elaborated, saying: "There are three duties implied in filial piety. They are:

"Serve your parents with full propriety, *li*, while they are alive.

"Bury them with full propriety when they die.

"Thereafter, visit their graves regularly, and show your respect by conducting the rites of propriety without fail." (2.5)

Student Meng's son asked about filial piety.

Confucius said: "Keep yourself in good health, so your parents need not worry about you." (2.6)

Student You asked about filial piety.

Confucius replied: "There is a general belief that, as long as you provide for your parents' material comfort you will have fulfilled your filial duties. But, you provide for your dogs and horses too. Without showing respect, there is no difference between providing for your parents and for your pets." (2.7)

Student Xia asked about filial piety.

Confucius replied: "Perhaps the most difficult part in serving your parents is to maintain a delightful heart and a happy mood while you attend to their needs and comply with their wishes. Answering to your parents' calls when they have something that needs doing, or presenting them with fine wine and good food, can hardly be regarded as fulfilling filial responsibilities." (2.8)

Confucius said: "I spent a whole day talking to my student Hui. He made no remark, nor asked any question, as if he were dull. But, as I observed him later, I became convinced that he was a good listener and learner, for he carried out what had been taught. Hui is not dull." (2.9)

Confucius said: "See what a person does, analyze his motives, and examine how he finds his peace of mind. With all these being transparent, his true character could not be concealed." (2.10)

Confucius said: "Acquire new knowledge on the foundation of what is already known. Such a habit will enable you to be your own teacher." (2.11)

Confucius said: "A gentleman keeps a broad outlook and a keen, inquisitive mind. He is not confined as a utensil." (2.12)

Student Gong asked what it takes to be a gentleman.

Confucius replied: "He tests his ideas in action before he expresses them in words." (2.13)

Confucius said: "A gentleman serves a community as a whole, making no differentiation.

"On the other hand, a base man is set on differentiating his own interest, thus losing sight of the community." (2.14)

Confucius said: "Learning without deliberation will lead to bewilderment.

"Deliberation without learning will result in jeopardy." (2.15)

Confucius said to student You: "Let me teach you what knowledge is.

"When you know a thing, hold on to it.

"When you are confused, admit that you do not know.

"That is true knowledge." (2.17)

Confucius said: "A man who is not trustworthy will not succeed in life, just like a cart without a crossbar cannot be pulled forward...." (2.22)

Confucius said: "To pay respect to the spirit of an unworthy dead is flattery.

"To refrain from doing a righteous act is cowardice." (2.24)

Confucius said: "How can a man who is not benevolent perform the rites of propriety?

"How can a man who is not benevolent perform fine music?" (3.3)

Student Lin asked about the true nature of *li*, propriety.

Confucius replied: "... For festivity rites, it is better to be frugal than extravagant.

"When mourning, it is better to grieve quietly than to attend to elaborate ceremonial rituals." (3.4)

Confucius said: "A gentleman has no contention except for a game of archery.

"On such an occasion, the gentleman would bow to his opponent to let him go first.

"Then, after the competition, the winner will bow to the loser to show respect, and offer him a glass of wine.

"This is the way when gentlemen compete." (3.7)

Student Xia asked: "A poem in the *Book of Poetry* says, 'Her cute smile accentuates the sweetness of her dimples. Her beautiful eyes emit clear definition of black and white. What is plain appears colorful.' Why is it so?"

Confucius replied: "Artists always put color onto a plain background."

Xia turned a twist to ask: "Could we appropriately say that loyalty and trust together constitute the plain background on which propriety adds the color for a character to shine?"

Confucius was delighted. He said: "You have a way of inspiring me. We can now go full force to learn how to appreciate the *Book of Poetry*." (3.8)

Confucius said: "We must honor our ancestors and gods as if they were present with us. If I cannot conduct the rites of worship in person, but ask others to represent me, then it will not be a show of *li*, propriety at all." (3.12)

Confucius lamented: "The music named *Shao* is absolutely beautiful and also absolutely good. But the music named *Wu* is only beautiful; it lacks perfection in goodness." (3.25)

Confucius said: "A community is good when its people practice *ren*, benevolence. A wise person knows this and chooses to live in just such a community." (4.1)

Confucius said: "People who do not exemplify the benevolent spirit are less able to endure poverty and hardship, and enjoy sustaining happiness.

"A benevolent man finds satisfaction in his belief.

"A wise man promotes benevolence to others whenever he can." (4.2)

Confucius said: "Only those who harbor the benevolent spirit can love other people, and to rebuke those who do evil." (4.3)

Confucius said: "A man bent on practicing the benevolent spirit is free from evil influences." (4.4)

Confucius said: "Wealth and honor are normal human desires. However, one should not acquire them in ways which deviate from virtuous principles.

"Poverty and lowliness are normal human aversions. But one should not avoid them by immoral means.

"A man whose behavior deviates from *ren*, the principle of benevolence, does not deserve to be called a gentleman.

"A gentleman does not behave in ways contrary to *ren* even for a moment, whether in times of difficulty, or in times of ease." (4.5)

Confucius said: "I have not encountered anyone who loves *ren*, nor have I seen one who dislikes the opposite of *ren*. Those who love *ren* exalt it above anything else. Those who dislike evil practice it without being affected by anything that is its opposite.

"Is there anyone able to practice *ren* for an entire day?

"I do not believe that there are people who lack the ability to behave in benevolent ways. If there are, I have yet to encounter them." (4.6)

Confucius said: "People are at fault for many different reasons, or their faults arise from different circumstances, not easily identified or explained.

"However, by observing the way a person faults, we can detect whether he bears the spirit of benevolence in his heart, or not." (4.7)

Confucius said: "Anyone who has recognized the right way of life in the morning can die with no regret by that same evening." (4.8)

Confucius said: "A scholar who is determined to seek truth, but is ashamed of his inferior clothes and food, is not qualified to participate in the discourse on truth." (4.9)

Confucius said: "There are no set ways of approaching or refusing any task in the world. A gentleman engaged in a task of *yi*, righteousness, approaches it according to emergent circumstances." (4.10)

Confucius said: "A gentleman cherishes virtue, while a base man cherishes earthly pleasure.

"A gentleman is mindful of the sanctions of law as he behaves, while a base man is keen on getting favors." (4.11)

Confucius said: "A person bent on seeking favors will invite complaints." (4.12)

Confucius said: "Do not be concerned whether you could obtain a good career position; prepare yourself that you may do well in one.

"Do not be concerned that you are not widely known, do your best to make a significant achievement so that you may deserve a popular acclaim." (4.14)

Once, Confucius murmured to his student Zeng that he held a single, pervading principle to guide his life.

After he left the classroom, the other students asked Zeng to explain the meaning of that statement.

Zeng said: "The principle that our teacher propounds embraces two concepts, that of loyalty, and that of forgiveness." (4.15)

Confucius said: "A gentleman knows and is obligated by *yi*, the principle of righteousness.

"A base man knows only gain." (4.16)

Confucius said: "When you encounter a man of ability and integrity, you should will yourself to learn from him and emulate those good qualities.

"When you encounter a man of dubious character, it is time to reflect on your own shortcomings." (4.17)

Confucius said: "Once we discover our parents engaged in doing wrong, we should tell them that they are wrong, genially and tactfully.

"If our parents insist that they are right, then, as sons and daughters, we should continue to respect them instead of antagonizing them.

"Even if our parents responded to our honest advice with anger, we should continue to love them." (4.18)

Confucius said: "Remember your parents' age well. Rejoice that they are living as long as they are, and be concerned that they are becoming weaker, as well as getting on in age." (4.21)

Confucius said: "People of bygone ages did not express themselves openly, for fear they might not be able to match their claims with appropriate deeds." (4.22)

Confucius said: "Cautious people will seldom err." (4.23)

Confucius said: "A gentleman says little and acts surely and swiftly." (4.24)

Confucius said: "A virtuous man is never isolated. He will surely be accompanied by like-minded people settling in his neighborhood." (4.25)

Student You said: "Remonstrating your superior repeatedly may lead to disgrace.

"Counseling your friends repeatedly may result in their alienation from you." (4.26)

Gongye Zhang was once chained and jailed in his home town. Confucius examined his case and concluded that he did not commit the crime that led to his imprisonment.

Confucius gave Gongye his own daughter's hand in marriage, declaring that he was a good man. (5.1)

Confucius praised his student Nan Rong saying: "He served his country under good governance, and managed to avoid trouble and punishment when corruption prevailed."

Confucius gave him his own niece's hand in marriage. (5.2)

Student Gong asked his teacher for an evaluation so he might know where he stood.

"You are like utensils," replied Confucius.

"What kind of utensils?" asked Gong.

"One decorated with gems, and used for sacrificial rites in our tradition," concluded Confucius. (5.4)

Someone referred to student Yong as kind, deep in *ren* spirit, but inarticulate.

Confucius retorted: "Why would he need to be articulate? I am not sure whether he is really virtuous. But why would he need to be articulate?" (5.5)

Confucius said: "Since not many people here accept my *dao*, my vision on life, I might as well board a raft to float about on the open sea. Maybe my student Lu would gladly accompany me."

Lu was openly elated on hearing his teacher's suggestion, unaware that his teacher was setting up a trap to test him.

Confucius then said: "This young man Lu is bolder than me. What he needs is better judgment." (5.7)

Student Meng asked Confucius if student Lu was a man of *ren*, benevolent spirit.

Confucius replied: "I am not sure."

Meng repeated his question to press for a definite answer.

Confucius said: "He could do well managing military affairs in a country of a thousand chariots. But I am not sure whether he is benevolent."

Meng then asked about another student Qiu.

Confucius said: "He is suited to be mayor of a city with one thousand families, or an estate with one hundred chariots. But I am not sure whether he is benevolent."

Meng continued to ask about Chi.

Confucius said: "He could do well wearing his ceremonial gown smartly tied up with a sash, walking about in a court relating to visitors. But I am not sure whether he is benevolent." (5.8)

Confucius asked his student Gong how he would compare himself with his classmate Hui.

Gong replied: "How dare I compare myself with him. He hears a statement from you and extrapolates to understand the whole lesson, whereas I may be able to know only one or two steps beyond what you have said."

Confucius concluded: "Yes, you are indeed not equal to

Hui. But I appreciate your honest assessment of yourself. And that is what is good about you." (5.9)

When Confucius saw his student Zai asleep in broad daylight he commented: "Rotten wood is not fit to be carved, just as a wall built with mud and dung is unworthy of whitewashing. For a man like Zai, there is no use for me to reprove him."

Later, Confucius reflected thus: "There was a time when I would give a person credit just by hearing his words. Now, I would listen to him, observe his behavior, then make a judgment on his character. It is Zai who has taught me this wisdom." (5.10)

Once, Confucius muttered, "I have yet to come across a person with an unbending will."

Thereupon someone suggested student Cheng as an example.

Confucius said, "Cheng is a man of excessive ambition, how can he be regarded as one with an unbending will?" (5.11)

Student Gong said to his teacher: "Just as I do not wish people to force me to do what I do not like, so I do not wish to force people to do what they do not like."

Confucius replied; "Gong, that is exactly the essence of *ren*. But that is not your attainment yet." (5.12)

Student Gong said: "Our teacher's interpretations of ancient writings are clear to us. However, his views on human nature and the way of Heaven still remain a mystery." (5.13)

Student Gong asked why Kong Wen Tze was posthumously awarded the title of *wen*.

Confucius explained: "He was a person whose high intellect was matched by his devotion to learning. He also was not ashamed to ask and learn from people inferior to him. Hence his posthumous title of *wen*." (5.15)

Confucius said: "The scholar Yan excelled in the art of human relations. However long he was acquainted with a person, he maintained the same respect for him." (5.17)

Confucius heard that the scholar Ji Wen would deliberate thrice before doing anything. He commented: "It is enough to deliberate twice." (5.20)

With the students Yan and Ji by his side, Confucius said: "Why not let each of us express his cherished wishes?"

Ji said: "I wish to have horses and carts, as well as light fur coats, so I can share them with my friends, and not to regret when such things are spoiled."

Yan said: "I wish I would never boast about what I can do well, or hide what I am unable to do."

When it was his turn, Confucius said: "I wish that the seniors in our community may live with dignity and tranquility; that friends will trust and help one another; and that our young may receive love and protection from their elders." (5.26)

Confucius once lamented: "Alas! I have yet to come across any person who is able to detect his own faults and, at the same time, to reflect on such faults with a view to rectifying them." (5.27)

Confucius said: "In any community of ten families, there would be someone as loyal and honest as me. However, there may not be anyone who would love learning to the extent that I do." (5.28)

Duke Ai asked Confucius which of his students loved learning most.

Confucius replied: "There was Hui. He loved to learn for its own sake, he did not pass his anger on to others, and he never committed the same mistake twice. Unfortunately, he died young. Now that he is gone, I have yet to find a person who loves learning as he did." (6.3)

Confucius said: "My student Hui was a good man. He lived contentedly in a small hut in a back alley, ate his rice in a bamboo bowl, and quenched his thirst with a gourd of plain water. Many people could not endure such hardship. But Hui felt happy just the same. Admirable indeed was Hui the good man." (6.11)

Student Ran once declared: "It is not that I do not appreciate my teacher's way of life, *dao*, I simply do not have the facility to follow it practically."

Confucius said to him: "If it was a matter of not having the appropriate facility to live my way of life, one would at least try until one had failed. In your case, you had not even taken a single step." (6.12)

Confucius advised his student Xia: "Be a good learner like a man of principle, and not one motivated by material rewards like a base man." (6.13)

Confucius said: "Who can go outside of a house to breathe the open air without passing through a door? Why then do people not follow my way of benevolence?" (6.17)

Confucius said: "A gentleman must maintain a balance between his natural ability and his literary achievement.... For, when his achievement does not measure up to his ability, he will be an underachiever; and when his ability is not matched by appropriate achievement, his is only marking his time like a clerk toiling on mundane chores." (6.18)

Confucius said: "A person's life is given meaning by integrity. If he should live without it, his is an existence of luck." (6.19)

Confucius said: "To love truth and goodness is better than to know about them. To take pleasure in living out the principles of truth and goodness is even more profound." (6.20)

Confucius said: "A teacher may successfully engage a student of above-average intelligence in discourses of high principles. He will have difficulties in doing so with one of below-average intelligence." (6.21)

Student Fan asked about the constitution of wisdom.

Confucius said: "Aspects of wisdom include serving others in virtuous ways, respecting the call of spirituality, and distancing oneself from unsound beliefs."

Fan asked about *ren*, the spirit of benevolence.

Confucius replied: "A benevolent person will give top priority to solving difficult problems as he encounters them, and worry about gains or merit afterward." (6.22)

Confucius said: "A wise man delights in keeping company with water.

"A benevolent person delights in admiring hills.

"The wise are active while the benevolent are tranquil.

"The wise are happy while the benevolent live long lives." (6.23)

Student Zai asked: "Would a benevolent man, when told about it, rush to rescue a person who had fallen into a well in order to prove his kindness?"

Confucius replied: "How can you raise such a question? A gentleman may attempt a rescue when informed of danger, but he will not risk his life just because he was told about it. He may be moved to act swiftly, but he will not be unjustifiably tricked by other people's opinion." (6.26)

Confucius said: "A gentleman equips himself with extensive knowledge about virtue, and keeps his behavior under the principles of propriety.

"In the same vein, he will not go astray by overstepping the boundaries of our fine tradition." (6.27)

Confucius said: "Perfect is the wisdom of *The Mean and Constancy*! It is regrettable that people have ceased practicing it for such a long while." (6.29)

Student Gong asked if a person could be called benevolent by giving extensively to benefit everyone.

Confucius replied: "His were not just actions of benevolence, but those of a sage, possibly beyond the legendary Yao and Shun.

"What is benevolence but that, when you wish to perfect yourself, take action to help others to perfect themselves first; and when you wish to communicate your thoughts, help others to do so before you do.

"Remember, the most effective way to practice the principles of benevolence is to appreciate the needs of other people as you do your own, and to empower others just as you would yourself." (6.30)

Confucius said: "I transmit traditional wisdom and do not create new ideas, because I admire and believe in the experiences and insights of our ancestors. I am a follower of the venerable scholar Peng of the Shang dynasty." (7.1)

Confucius said: "I examine myself often to see if I have done any of the following:

- Quietly accumulating knowledge in the hope of gaining insight.
- Doing my studies, undisturbed by outside annoyance.
- Teaching untiringly." (7.2)

Confucius said: "I have grave concerns about any shortcomings that I have in these areas:

- Not adequately cultivating traditional values.
- Not thoroughly discussing what I have learned.
- Not being able to practice *yi*, righteous principles, even when I know them.
- Not being able to change what is not good in my own character." (7.3)

Confucius said: "I must be old and feeble. I have not dreamed of the Duke of Zhou lately." (7.5)

Confucius said: "Remember to live in accordance with *dao*, the way of life.
    "Stand firm in your understanding of virtue.
    "Adhere to the principles of benevolence, *ren*.
    "Engage in learning the art of rites, music, archery, driving, and arithmetic." (7.6)

Confucius said: "I have never turned away a student who came to my door, even if the fee he had brought was meager." (7.7)

Confucius said: "I will not teach anyone before he has made a good effort to learn but failed to understand.

"I do not repeat my teaching for a student who, after seeing my demonstration on an angle of a subject matter, could not extrapolate to understand the remaining three." (7.8)

Confucius would never eat his fill in the presence of mourners. Nor would he sing on the same day that he had wept in sorrow. (7.9–10)

Confucius once heard a piece of music named *Shao* in the State of Qi. He was so overwhelmed by its exquisite beauty that, in the ensuing three months, he was unable to sense the taste of meat.

He said afterward that he was hitherto unaware of such power in music in touching the human soul. (7.14)

Confucius said: "I could be happy if I had to eat coarse rice, drink plain water, and sleep on a pillow formed by my own bended arm. To me, riches are as light as a floating cloud, if they are obtained by unrighteous means." (7.16)

Confucius said: "If I was given a few more years of life so that

I could study the *Book of Changes* at the age of fifty, I might be freed from major faults." (7.17)

Poetry, history, and the practice of propriety are the most frequently discussed topics in Confucius' teachings. (7.18)

The Duke of Ye asked student Lu about his teacher and was given no reply.

On leaning about it later, Confucius told Lu: "Why? You could have said that my teacher is a simple man. He often skipped his meals when engaged in deep studies. He would allow the joy of discovering new knowledge to eclipse any feeling of remorse. He is so absorbed in the pleasure of learning that he is unaware of getting old." (7.19)

Confucius said: "I am not a born knower. What knowledge I have is the outcome of my love for antiquity and tradition, and my zest in pursuing what other people had known." (7.20)

Confucius said: "When I walk with two other men, I know that one of them could be my teacher.

"I should therefore try to learn from the better of the two, and venture to help the remaining one to improve himself." (7.22)

Confucius usually taught four subjects: arts and letters, behavior and character formation, loyalty to self and others, and trust and obligations. (7.25)

Confucius fishes not with a net; nor does he shoot a perching bird. (7.27)

Confucius said: "People might do things without knowing, but I do not. Be prepared to listen widely, and to follow your chosen way.

"It is also important to observe extensively how experts work, and to benefit from the experience.

"In so doing, you might not understand everything thoroughly, but your knowledge is second only to that of people who knew from first-hand experience." (7.28)

Confucius said: "The spirit of benevolence dwells in everyone's heart. It is therefore not remote and difficult to reach.

"When I wish to seek *ren*, lo, it emerges readily in my heart." (7.30)

Confucius was singing with friends.

Whenever someone sang well, he would ask for an encore, then invite him to do a duet together. (7.32)

Confucius said: "I may compare equally with any other man in arts and letters. However, when it comes to practicing what one knows about virtue and morality, such as expected of a gentleman, I cannot say I am doing well." (7.33)

Once, Confucius was very sick, and his student Lu asked to pray for him.

"Is there such an act?" asked Confucius.

"Yes," replied Lu, who continued and explained, "According to the *Lei Prayers*, if I can convince the gods up in Heaven and here on Earth to right your wrongs, you may be healed."

"If that is what you intend to do, I have been doing it all the time," reminded the Master, who showed that he was still very sick. (7.35)

Confucius said: "Being overly extravagant is showing off beyond the rules of *li*, propriety.

"Being overly frugal may be construed as being mean.

"On balance, it is better to be frugal." (7.36)

Confucius said: "The gentleman is openly happy and accomplished. The base man is in duress." (7.37)

Confucius is gentle yet stern.

He is authoritative yet undemanding.

He is humble and tranquil. (7.38)

Confucius said: "Paying respect without the modulation of *li* is only being busy.

"Being cautious without the modulation of *li* is timid.

"Acting boldly without the modulation of *li* becomes insubordinate.

"Acting intuitively without the modulation of *li* could be considered rude.

"When high-ranking officials revere their elders, commoners may be inspired to espouse the spirit of benevolence, *ren*.

"When high-ranking officials keep their old friends and colleagues in their hearts, ordinary folks will not be mean to one another." (8.2)

Student Meng visited his classmate Zeng who fell ill. The latter said: "When a bird is about to die, its chirps are sad, just as when a man is about to die, his words are kind. I can say to you that a gentleman who cares about virtue should be mindful of three issues. They are:

- To maintain good deportment always, thus distancing himself from violence and unruly behavior.
- To wear a warm smile always, thus projecting a trusting attitude.
- To speak from the heart so people will sense neither impropriety nor aloofness.

"As for such mundane matters as correctly handling the sacrificial vessels, they could be taken care of by clerks who specialized in such acts." (8.4)

Student Zeng remembered his classmate Hui and praised him thus: "Although he was gifted and able, he strove to learn from people who knew less than him.

"Although his knowledge was extensive and profound, he often asked to learn from people who knew little.

"Though he possessed a lot, he believed he was inadequate.

"Solidly endowed and accomplished, he appeared to be empty.

"He would not rebuke people who offended him. That was my friend Hui." (8.5)

Student Zeng said: "A scholar bears a heavy responsibility along a lengthy course. He should therefore cultivate strong resilience and perseverance in himself.

"His responsibility is heavy because he is committed to promoting the spirit of benevolence, *ren*. His course is long because such a commitment is lifelong." (8.7)

Confucius said: "Poetry nurtures good hearts. Propriety, *li*, helps to establish fine character. Music promotes beneficial accomplishment." (8.8)

Confucius said: "People may be guided to follow a set of disciplinary rules, but no education is adequate in helping them to do so on their own initiatives." (8.9)

Confucius said: "Society will become disrupted and chaotic if people are bitter with poverty and quick to act.

"In the same vein, when people are consumed by primitive wants and care little about *ren*, social order will be under threat." (8.10)

Confucius said: "He who firmly believes in virtue and commits himself to learning more about it throughout life ... will avail himself of the opportunity to promote moral principles under a good government. He would recede into oblivion at times of social disarray.

"When a country is governed with strong moral principles, poverty and dishonor are objects of social shame.

"When a country is governed with an absence of moral principles, wealth and honor will become objects of social shame." (8.13)

Confucius said: "When he was in charge of musical affairs, Maestro Zhi incorporated passages from the poem *Guan Ju* with majestic tunes, bringing great pleasure to everyone's heart." (8.15)

Confucius said: "I have little understanding of or sympathy for people who are high in ambition but low in moral principle; who are ignorant but unwilling to learn, and whose ability is ordinary yet whose promises are unreliable." (8.16)

Confucius said: "Do learn with a full commitment, as if you are inadequate and concerned about losing all that you already know." (8.17)

Confucius seldom used the word profitability in his teachings. When he did, it was invariably discussed relative to the givens of life and the spirit of love and caring, *ren*. (9.1)

Once, a neighbor made this comment: "Confucius is great. His knowledge is broad. But he has no specialty to show for fame."

On hearing about it Confucius said in front of his students: "What should I specialize in? In driving a chariot? Or in archery? Maybe I will specialize in chariot driving." (9.2)

Confucius said: "As specified in the protocol of traditional ceremonies, a participant should wear a hat made of threads of jute. Today, people choose to wear hats of silk for economy. I follow the trend.

"In traditional protocol, one pays respect to the venerable authority, bowing from below the steps leading to his house. Today, people choose to bow to him in the hall where he sits, showing inadequate respect. I still make my bows from below the steps, even when this shows that I am against the trend." (9.3)

Confucius guards himself absolutely against four inclinations, namely:

- Holding a preconceived idea.
- Making an exclusive conclusion.
- Being inflexible.
- Being egoistic. (9.4)

The people of Kuang said that they feared Confucius as they did the tiger.

Confucius responded: "After the death of Emperor Wen, the legacy of his *li* and *yue*, propriety and music, was passed on to me.

"If it were the will of Heaven that this cultural heritage should vanish, then we, the inheritors, could abstain from playing a part in it.

"However, if it were Heaven's will that it should flourish without interruption, then, even the people of Kuang cannot stop me from resolutely promoting it." (9.5)

An officer of high rank once asked student Gong: "Is your Master a sage, being so able and knowledgeable?"

Gong said: "He is a sage because Heaven has so boundlessly endowed him with wisdom. His high ability and extensive knowledge are of secondary importance."

When Confucius learned about his student's comments, he said: "How could this man know about me? I was born with very little means. So it was necessary for me to learn the basic skills of survival early in life. If you ask me whether a gentleman should have all these mundane skills, I would say, only some of them."

Then, a student named Lao commented: "Teacher, did you not once say that you were able to devote a lot of time to learning because you were not appointed to high office?" (9.6)

Confucius said: "Do I possess a lot of knowledge? No. When an ordinary man approached me with a question that I knew little about, I would examine it from the beginning to the end, and then let him on to what I had discovered." (9.8)

Student Hui once murmured these comments in exultation: "My teacher teaches me logic and methodology. He first taught me to make extensive references, then how to organize information in the context of *li*, propriety, and to pursue truth untiringly. At some point in my learning process, I seemed to have seen him standing just in front of me. But, whenever I tried to catch up with him, I found I was lagging far behind.

"His visions were profound that they foresaw what was to come. But they were all anchored solidly in the depth of our tradition." (9.11)

Once, when Confucius fell seriously ill, his student Lu ordered the servants to prepare for his funeral, and acted as if he was the master of ceremonies.

Later, Confucius got well. He declared that Lu was both wrong and deceitful, saying: "There was no need to pretend that I had a master of ceremonies when I had none. Who are we trying to fool? Could it be Heaven? In fact, I would rather die with a few of my students attending than to die in the company of these pretenders. In that way, I would die unadorned by an elaborate burial, a step further from falling on the roadside." (9.12)

Confucius once declared that he wished to go east to live among the people of nine primitive tribes.

A student said: "Why would our teacher wish to live with those primitive people? They are uncultured and rude."

Confucius asked: "When a gentleman dwells there with them, would they still be uncultured?" (9.14)

Confucius declared: "I returned to Lu to restore music and the arts in their proper places. You can now see that the *Ya Poems* and the *Zong Songs* are established in their rightful positions." (9.15)

Once, Confucius was standing by the bank of a river watching the currents flow. He murmured: "Human affairs are like rushing water, which toils on unceasingly, irrespective of day or night." (9.17)

Confucius once said: "I have not encountered anyone who loved virtue as passionately as he did beauty." (9.18)

Confucius said: "Learning may be compared to piling waste to build a mount, its height is not achieved if one stops half-way, or spare a last basket of earth.

"Learning may be compared with building on flat land; positive results can be seen with each successive effort." (9.19)

Confucius praised his favorite student Hui: "My student Hui never hesitated to learn whenever I set him up for it. He habitually pursued his learning till he had attained full understanding, never stopping in the process. Alas, how unfortunate that he died so young!" (9.21)

Confucius said: "We must respect the younger generation. What they can achieve could very well surpass what exists today.

"However, if a man has not shown any distinguished accomplishment by age forty or fifty, not much could be said about him." (9.23)

Confucius said: "Can a student who has made a mistake benefit from a disciplinary action? It would be better if he was helped to correct the mistake.

"Would a student not be pleased to receive useful advice? It would be better if he followed the advice to improve his learning.

"A teacher can do little to help if a student accepted his advice but did nothing to benefit from it; or, if he showed delight with the suggested approach but took no action to understand its facilitative intent." (9.24)

Confucius said: "One could subjugate the commander of a large army, yet, one can never bend the will of a common man." (9.26)

Confucius said: "My student You could be the only person who would, with his usual cotton attire, feel no shame as he mingled among people clothed in fur." (9.27)

Confucius said: "It is the test of a harsh winter that showed the resilience of pines and cypresses." (9.28)

Confucius said: "A knower knows no perplexity, a benevolent person entertains no anxiety, a courageous person has no fear." (9.29)

Confucius said: "People who study together may not share the same values.

"People who share the same values may not practice them in the same ways.

"People who practice the same principles may not apply them in different situations so as to attain the most benefits from them." (9.30)

Once, some students hinted to Confucius of his aloofness toward them by citing an old poem: "Even cherry blooms flutter, as if moved by emotions. How can we not think of you? Only that you are standing so far away."

Confucius replied: "Maybe you did not think of me earnestly enough? If you keep me close to your hearts, how can I be far away?" (9.31)

Confucius regarded eating as an important aspect of life, placing health above all else.

He liked to eat finely cooked food, with meat cut in small pieces for easy consumption.

He would not eat burned rice, stale fish and meat, or anything that was discolored, smelling bad, or poorly cooked.

He preferred fruits and vegetables that were ripened in season, and meat cut properly and seasoned with appropriate herbs and sauces.

He ate sparingly, making sure that the amount of meat in a meal did not exceed that of rice.

There was no specified limit for wine, except that one must not get drunk.

He would not refuse ginger in food because of its medicinal value.

Talking was not allowed while eating. And he would not speak while in bed.

He always offered food to honor his ancestors. Such food might be simple. But it was offered with great respect. (10.8)

Confucius said: "People who understood music and ceremonial rites before they were appointed to office were seen as rustics.

"Nowadays, gentlemen from well-to-do families were appointed to office and they knew the forms rather than substance of music and rites.

"I prefer to appoint people from the first group." (11.1)

Confucius said: "Students who had accompanied me in Chen and Cai are no longer with me now. Among them, Hui, Min, Ran, and Zhong were very strong in moral character. Zai and Gong were excellent at speech. You and Xia were best at literary studies. For administration, Ran and Zi surpassed everyone." (11.2–3)

Confucius said: "Hui was of little help to me in advancing my studies. He readily agreed with all that I taught, and did not express his views at any time." (11.4)

Confucius said: "Min is a son of real filial piety and affection, as attested by the praises of his parents and brothers and sisters." (11.5)

Nan Rong frequently recited the poem *Bai Gui* (white jade scepter). It says that, while a black spot on a white scepter stone could be removed on demand, words that hurt people could not be retracted once they were spoken.

Confucius was so impressed that he gave Nan Rong his niece's hand in marriage. (11.6)

Confucius' friend Ji Kang asked him which one of his students loved learning the most.

He replied: "Hui. It is unfortunate that he died young. No one could fit that description now." (11.7)

Upon student Hui's death, his father begged Confucius to sell his carriage and used the money to buy a coffin shell for the burial.

Confucius responded: "Every father loves his son as much as any other father. When my son Li died, he was buried in a coffin without a shell. I did not sell my carriage to buy the shell for him because I needed my carriage for travel, as demanded by social customs for a man of my stature." (11.8)

Upon Hui's death, Confucius was so sad that he lamented repeatedly: "Heaven shows no mercy on me, Heaven shows no mercy on me." (11.9)

Confucius wailed with great sorrow at the death of Hui.

His students pleaded him to contain his grief.

He said: "My grief is not enough. If I do not grieve for Hui, whom could I grieve for?" (11.10)

After Hui died, a few of his classmates wished to give him an elaborate burial.

Confucius advised that they should not do so.

The classmates went ahead anyway, and buried Hui elaborately.

Confucius said: "In life, Hui treated me like I was his father, but I could not treat him like my son. Now, I cannot even keep his burial in line with the prescribed rites of *li*, propriety. The fault is not in me, but in the few of you." (11.11)

Student Lu asked about the proper way of treating the ghost and the gods.

Confucius advised: "When you do not serve man respectfully enough, what is the point in seeking ways to serve the dead?"

Lu then asked if a dead man turns into a ghost.

Confucius advised: "Since we know little about life, how could we fathom the mystery of death?" (11.12)

Once, Confucius was in a contented mood observing his favorite students around him. Min was by his side, virtuous and humble. Lu portrayed a confident and motivated stance. Ran and Gong looked sincere and simple. The Master was pleased.

Then, he turned to Lu with a special piece of advice: "If you keep on being driven by excessive self-confidence, I fear that you might die an unnatural death." (11.13)

The State of Lu was tearing down its traditional treasury building in order to build a new one.

Student Min commented: "Could they not renovate the original building since it is still solid and spacious?"

Confucius praised: "This man speaks sparingly. However, when he does, he is always right on the dot." (11.14)

Once, on hearing student You playing the lute, Confucius thought the music lacked the harmonic tune that he had taught.

The other students began to look down on You when they became aware of Confucius' appraisal.

Confucius then cleared their doubts. He said: "You is already in my lounge, though he has yet to enter my inner chamber." (11.15)

Student Gong asked his teacher which one of the two students, Shi or Shang, is superior in talent and virtue.

Confucius replied: "Shi's ambitions are high and extensive, while Shang remains cautious and humble as he relates to people."

Gong was quick to conclude that Shang was a better man.

Confucius then corrected him, saying: "One could be just as wrong to go beyond as to remain static." (11.16)

The Ji family was richer than the Duke of Zhou. When Confucius became aware that his student Qui was assisting the Jis to widen their interests and wealth, he was furious.

He then told his other students that Qui was not qualified to be his student anymore, and urged everyone to assail him as loudly as they could. (11.17)

Confucius gave his students the following appraisals: Chai was slow and clumsy, Shen could not learn effectively, Shi was specious, but You was well informed. (11.18)

Confucius said: "Hui was poor and constantly in need. But his conduct was perfectly virtuous. Ci did not acquiesce in his given lot. He went into business to try his talent, showing consistent sound judgment." (11.19)

Student Zhang asked about the characteristics of a good person.

Confucius replied: "He does not have to follow the footsteps of others. Nor does he have to enter the chamber of the sages." (11.20)

Student Lu asked his teacher whether one should immediately get involved to do a good thing when presented with the opportunity.

Confucius advised: "You have your father and brother at home. You should consult them before you commit yourself."

Student Ran asked the same question, and Confucius advised: "Of course, you should waste no time to get involved."

Another student Gongxi was perplexed, and inquired why the same question was met with two different answers.

Confucius explained: "Ran was timid and reserved, so I pushed him forward. But Lu was a go-getter, I therefore held him back a little." (11.22)

Student Ji asked Confucius if either Zhong or Ran was ready to serve as minister for state affairs.

Confucius replied: "A minister is required to serve his king according to the principles of virtue. He should resign when he is prevented from doing so. Now, both Zhong and Ran could do well as civil servants."

"You mean they will follow orders resolutely?" asked Ji.

"Not if they were ordered to kill their father or king," replied Confucius. (11.24)

Once, student Lu helped his classmate Gao to be appointed a provincial Governor.

On hearing about it, Confucius told Lu: "You are ruining the life of someone's son!"

Lu countered: "Why must excellence be achieved only through studying the books? This job will provide Gao with opportunities to serve his people and society, and learn from the process."

Confucius was vexed. He said: "I dislike the arrogance of an impolite man!" (11.25)

One day, sitting relaxed with his students, Confucius noticed their reticence and said: "Come, forget our age difference, let's take turns to tell what each one of us would do if our wishes were fulfilled."

Student Lu volunteered in haste: "I could reverse the ill fate of a state of ten thousand chariots, even when it was threatened by the armed advances of its strong neighbor, and its people were suffering from a severe famine. I would turn things around in three years if given the responsibility of governance. People would then be motivated to work and try their hand at creating. They would also follow the rules of righteousness in whatever they do."

Confucius grinned.

Ran signaled to speak. He said: "If I was appointed to govern a state of fifty to seventy square *li* (Chinese mile), I would spend three years to provide the people with abundant food and other necessary goods. But I do not have the ability to teach my people about propriety and music. I should like to leave that to talented gentlemen in the state."

Gongxi spoke next. He said: "I would be satisfied to be a minor officer in the civil service. I would then be able to learn to augment my limited ability. Perhaps I could serve a prince to prepare for his diplomatic meetings. I could also stand by him as he performs rites of respect in honor of his ancestors and the gods in the temple."

Confucius then turned to student Zeng who was playing the lute. He stopped instantly, laid the lute aside, and jerked out a note, saying: "My wishes are somewhat different.... On a sunny day in late spring, I would take five or six youths together with six or seven children wearing the right clothes, and wade into the shallow water by the bank of the Yi River. Afterward, we would take a short nap under the waving trees, allowing the natural breeze to brush our faces. Then, when we are ready to return home, we would trot along, singing our favorite tunes."

Confucius let out a long sigh of agreement, murmuring that his wishes were quite similar to Zeng's. (11.26)

Student Hui asked for an explanation of *ren*, benevolence.

Confucius said: "To subdue one's self-centered desires and to adhere to the traditional principles of *li*, propriety. Anyone who can achieve this in the course of a day will gain the love and respect of people within Heaven and Earth. They will identify with him and follow his role model in *ren*. Only the individual himself can inculcate the benevolent spirit. No one can do it for him."

Hui asked for the steps to be taken.

"Look not at what is in discord with propriety; hear not

what is in discord with propriety; speak not what is in discord with propriety; and act not what is in discord with propriety," replied Confucius.

Hui said: "Even though I cannot understand all that you have said because of my limited intelligence, I will follow these steps to the best of my ability." (12.1)

Student Zhong asked for an explanation of *ren*, benevolence.

Confucius said: "When you go abroad to do business, relate to people as if you were interacting with the most respected guests at home. When you engage people to work for you, do so with as much attention to dignity as if you were paying respect to your ancestors and gods. Keep this motto close to your heart all the time: Do not do to others what you would not wish them to do to you ... When you are acting on this motto, you will hear no complaint from anyone on Earth."

Zhong said: "Although I do not understand all that you have said because of my limited intelligence, I will live by this motto as best as I could." (12.2)

Student Si Ma asked for an explanation of *ren*.

Confucius said: "A benevolent man speaks guardedly, so he will not spread evil or hurt other people."

Si Ma said: "Is this it? You mean *ren* is simply to guard what one says?"

Confucius then said: "Yes, but it is easier said than done. So it is important to guard one's words." (12.3)

Student Si Ma asked his teacher to explain the concept of a gentleman.

Confucius said: "A gentleman worries not and fears not ... because he always reflects on what he has done, usually without regret." (12.4)

Student Si Ma spoke to his classmate Xia sadly: "Everyone has brothers and sisters but me."

Xia comforted him, saying: "Our teacher had once said that matters of life and death are predetermined in Heaven, as it is with wealth and satisfaction. A gentleman is predisposed to accept and respect the givens in life, and he treats others with propriety. Since people within the four seas are all brothers and sisters, how could a gentleman be concerned that he had no siblings in this world?" (12.5)

Student Zeng asked Confucius to explain vision.

Confucius replied: "When a person does not believe in flattery and he is unaffected by slander, and when he sees things clearly and in perspective, he can be called a visionary." (12.6)

Zhang asked his teacher to explain how to exalt virtue and identify delusion.

Confucius said: "To exalt virtue is to hold fast to faithfulness and trust, and test practice *yi*, the spirit of righteousness.

"You may love a person and wish him long life, you may hate a person and wish him dead. The fact that you wished individuals to be alive or dead, not knowing that these matters are predetermined, reflect your delusion." (12.10)

Confucius said: "A gentleman seeks to help other people to do their best, and to subdue their bad qualities.

"A base man seeks to do the opposite." (12.16)

Student Ji asked about good leadership.

"To lead means to rectify. If a leader exemplifies virtue, no one will dare not to practice virtue," replied Confucius. (12.17)

Student Ji asked about good governance and said: "How about implementing the death penalty to punish those who erred seriously and, at the same time, to warn everyone against sin?"

Confucius replied: "Why do you need the death penalty since you are already in governance? Evince your good deeds so as to set good examples for your people, and they will follow you in doing good.

"The virtue of a gentleman is like the wind, while the virtue of a base man is like grass. The grass will bend whenever and however the wind blows." (12.19)

Student Fan tagged along with Confucius as he roamed below the Rain Altar.

He asked his teacher how to exalt virtuous behavior, eliminate sinful acts, and recognize and be rid of delusion.

Confucius replied: "This is a good question. Do what is good and virtuous according to the commonly accepted principles, regardless of what your deeds would lead to.

"To be rid of one's delusions and wrongs, it is best to arrest one's own mistakes and sinful acts, instead of criticizing and dispelling the wicked actions of other people.

"If you treated your anger with no regard for your dignity and your parents' concerns, it would truly be a very big delusion." (12.21)

Student Fan asked Confucius to explain *ren*, benevolence.
"Love people," replied the teacher.
Fan asked about wisdom.
"Know people," replied the teacher.
Fan took leave, perplexed.
He met his classmate Xia a few days later, and shared his perplexity, saying: "When I showed my perplexity, our Master simply told me to respect and work with people who are upright, so the wicked will have no place to stand. Then, they will learn to be upright. What did it mean?"
Xia replied: "What the Master said was truly great. You see, the ancient Emperor Shun appointed Gaoyao to work with him, and all the wicked people disappeared. The great Tang did the same with the appointment of Yiyin, and achieved the same effect." (12.22)

Student Gong asked about friendship.
Confucius replied: "Admonish your friends whenever they are wrong, and help them to see the time-honored moral principles.
"However, if they do not heed your advice, do not press your views. You will avoid possible reprisals." (12.23)

Zeng said: "The gentleman associates himself with friends using word and literary narrations, thereby enhancing clear benevolent principles." (12.24)

Student Lu asked about the art of administration.

Confucius advised: "Work with people to set examples of good work habits."

Lu asked for more.

Confucius said: "Persist in doing the same." (13.1)

Student Fan asked Confucius about agriculture.

"I do not know as much about it as an experienced farmer," Confucius replied.

Fan then asked about vegetable cultivation.

Confucius gave a similar reply.

After Fan had left, Confucius made these remarks in front of his class: "Fan is small-minded indeed, especially when he had decided to be a leader.

"When a leader behaves according to propriety, his people will not dare to show him disrespect. When a leader acts according to righteous principles, his people will not dare to disobey. When a leader exalts trustworthiness, his people will not dare to forego their commitment.

"Provided that a leader adheres to these principles, people will flock to him from all directions, bringing their families to work with him. Would there be any need for the leader to grow crops?" (13.4)

Confucius said: "A man may be able to recite 300 poems. However, he may not be able to rule if called to govern a country. He may indeed not know how to convey the right message in a diplomatic mission. What is the use of knowing so many poems?" (13.5)

Confucius said: "When a leader exemplifies virtue, the people will function effectively without any decree.

"When a leader acts counter to virtue, no decree can effectively regulate the people." (13.6)

Confucius complimented the Duke of Jin on his wisdom in managing the wealth of his family, saying: "When they first had a simple house to live in, he said: 'We are now comfortable enough.'

"When the house was later enlarged, he said: 'We are now well endowed.'

"When the house became a mansion, he said: 'We are now perfectly satisfied.'" (13.8)

Student Ran drove Confucius' carriage as they went to visit the State of Wei.

They noticed that the economy there was quite good. Ran muttered that not much needed to be done for the people there.

"We can help them to become rich," said Confucius.

"Then, what?" asked Ran.

"Help them to become educated," concluded Confucius. (13.9)

Confucius said: "Even with the administration of an able and virtuous ruler, it would take the time of a generation for people to nurture the spirit of benevolence." (13.12)

Confucius said: "A leader would have no difficulty ruling his country effectively if he was upright.

"On the other hand, a leader who cannot exalt virtue will be unable to raise the moral standards of his people." (13.13)

The Duke of Ye asked Confucius to teach him good governance.

Confucius said: "Enable people near you to achieve happiness, then others will flock to you from afar." (13.16)

When student Xia was appointed county magistrate, he asked Confucius about good governance.

"Do not look for quick success, and do not vie for small advantages. He who is desirous of quick success will not reach his goals. He who loves small advantages will not achieve greatness." (13.17)

The Duke of Ye took great pride in informing Confucius: "People in my community are generally upright. There is the example of a man who volunteered to bear witness to the fact that his father had stolen a sheep."

Confucius countered: "We have a different expectation of a son in our community. Here, since a father would conceal his son's fault, the son is expected to do the same for his father. We call this uprightness." (13.18)

Student Fan asked about benevolence, *ren*.

Confucius said: "Be humble at home. Be cautious and respect-ful when doing business outside of home. Be loyal and trustworthy when relating with people. Even when you have gone to live in a foreign land, do not give up these rules and betray your values." (13.19)

Student Gong asked about the essential qualities of an officer.

Confucius said: "He knows shame as he behaves, and he will not disgrace his country as he leads a mission in a foreign country."

Gong asked: "What about that of a person for a lower position?"

Confucius said: "He is a loving and respectful son in his clan, and a caring and supportive brother in his village."

Gong asked: "What about a person who fits yet a lower office?"

Confucius said: "His words are trustworthy. His actions are resolute. He is a base man who follows orders dutifully. But he is nevertheless a petty officer."

Gong asked: "What is your opinion about our rulers today?"

Confucius said: "Oh, they are so short-sighted. They do not count much." (13.20)

Confucius said: "If I cannot befriend people who conform to conventions, I will associate myself with people who are progressive and genuine.

"The progressive will persist in moving forward and doing new things. The genuine will not do evil." (13.21)

Confucius said: "A gentleman will collaborate with others while maintaining a unique point of view.

"A base man will follow the crowd while disagreeing at heart." (13.23)

Student Gong asked his teacher: "How do you judge a person who is liked by everyone in his community?"

Confucius replied: "It is difficult to say."

"What about someone hated by all?" asked Gong.

Confucius replied: "Still hard to say. I would say a good person is liked by all the virtuous people in his community, and hated by all the bad ones." (13.24)

Confucius said: "A gentleman is easy to work with but difficult to please. He will not be pleased by deviant actions even when exercised with good intentions. But, he will assign people to do different jobs according to each person's ability.

"A base man is easy to please but difficult to work with. He will be pleased by any charming action, including deviant ones. But, when he assigns people to do different jobs, he demands perfection from everyone." (13.25)

Confucius said: "A gentleman is tranquil but not smug.

"A base man is smug but not tranquil." (13.26)

Confucius said: "A person who is resolute, persistent, modest, and cautious with words, is close to being benevolent." (13.27)

Student Lu asked about the requisite qualities of a gentleman.

Confucius said: "He must treat people sincerely and earnestly, affably and pleasantly. He will be caring and encouraging among friends, gentle and affectionate among brothers and sisters." (13.28)

Confucius said: "To lead an uninformed people to war is to abandon them." (13.30)

Confucius said: "A student who cherishes only sustaining pleasure is not fit to be a scholar." (14.2)

Confucius said: "A virtuous man is usually correct with words, but a man who is correct with words is not necessarily virtuous.

"A benevolent man is usually bold in action, but a bold man is not necessarily benevolent." (14.4)

Confucius said: "A gentleman could occasionally act contrary to benevolent principles.

"A base man will never act in tune with benevolent principles." (14.6)

Confucius said: "Can a father who loves his son not subject him to work?

"Can a minister loyal to his king not advise him of his wrongs?" (14.7)

Confucius said: "It is difficult for a poor man not to complain.

"It is easy for a rich man to refrain from showing arrogance." (14.10)

Student Lu asked about the perfect man.

Confucius said: "... A perfect man today need not possess those qualities as exemplified by the legendary kings and sages. If a man is mindful of righteousness when he encounters profit, if he is ready to make a sacrifice before danger, if he keeps a promise made long ago, he is a perfect man." (14.12)

Confucius said: "A gentleman improves his character every day.

"A base man tarnishes his character just as often." (14.23)

Confucius said: "Students in bygone days learned to improve their knowledge and moral conduct.

"Students today learn to seek other people's approval and praise." (14.24)

Confucius said: "A gentleman speaks cautiously, as if embarrassed about what he has to say. However, when he acts upon his words, he will do more than what he has said." (14.27)

Confucius said: "A gentleman's conduct has three dimensions; I fail in all of them. They are: being benevolent and free from anxiety, being wise and free from doubts, and being courageous and free from fear."

Student Gong said: "Master, you are being modest in what you said about yourself." (14.28)

Student Gong was fond of appraising other people.

Confucius said to him: "You must see perfection in yourself that you dare to appraise others. For me, I have no time to do that sort of thing." (14.29)

Confucius said: "Do not be concerned that others do not appreciate your capabilities.

"Be concerned that you do not have many." (14.30)

Confucius said: "A wise person does not suspect wild deceit on the part of others. Nor does he anticipate default any time. He knows intuitively that people could be trustworthy or deceptive." (14.31)

Someone asked Confucius: "What do you think of people who use virtue to respond to grievance?"

Confucius replied: "Then, how do these people respond to virtue? I believe that one should treat other people's grievance squarely, and use virtue to respond to virtue." (14.34)

Once, Confucius lamented: "Why is it that people do not understand me?"

"Why do you say so?" asked Gong.

Confucius continued: "I do not moan about what is given by Heaven, I do not grumble about people. I devote myself totally to studying man and his affairs, from the simplest to the most complex dimensions. God knows what I am trying to accomplish!" (14.35)

Confucius was beating his stone drum for pleasure one day.

A man carrying a straw basket passed by. He stopped to listen and muttered: "This drummer seems to be loaded down with a sense of public obligation. He seems bent on saving the whole world when, in fact, he is not understood nor recognized. He should accept his fate and rest his case."

Confucius heard the comment and said: "How perceptive is this man! I could follow his suggestions." (14.39)

Confucius said: "When the leader observes the principles of propriety, the people will follow and abide by the rules." (14.41)

Student Lu asked about the qualities of a gentleman.

Confucius said: "A gentleman perfects himself constantly so he can better respect others. He also perfects himself so he is able to help other people to achieve peace and happiness ..." (14.42)

One day, Confucius went to see his old friend Yuan Rang.

The latter received him sitting down, with his legs spread wide in a rude posture.

Confucius went forward to hit him with his walking stick and said: "You defied the rules of rites when you were young, you accomplished nothing in your adulthood, you keep on consuming in old age, unwilling to die; you are a liability to your community!" (14.43)

The Prince of Wei asked Confucius about war strategy.

Confucius replied that he had no such expertise, and left the state with his students the next day.

The entourage arrived at the State of Chen eventually. They no longer had any provisions left ... One of the students fell ill.

Student Lu was enraged, feeling that the world was not fair to his teacher. He lamented: "Is this the fate of a gentleman, the guardian of moral principles?"

Confucian remarked: "A gentleman committed to moral principles may suffer from poverty. A base man will resort to unlawful acts when saddled with poverty." (15.1–2)

Confucius asked Lu once: "Do you believe that I learn by storing bits and pieces of knowledge in my memory?"

"Yes, Master," replied Lu.

"That is not correct," said Confucius, "I hold fast to a set of principles, and then applied them to everything I come across in daily life." (15.3)

Student Zhang asked about how to behave so as to be respected in every situation.

Confucius replied: "Keep your words true and trustworthy, and conduct your affairs carefully and honorably. You will do well even in a savage land, north or south.

"On the other hand, if your words and actions were contrary to your promises, you will not be welcome even in your hometown.

"So, when you are standing, see these principles as if they were posted in front of you. When you are riding in your carriage, remember them as if they were attached to the yoke of your horse. You will then be successful wherever you roam."

Zhang was so impressed with these words that he had them written on his belt. (15.6)

Confucius said: "To fail to communicate with people who can share good values with you is a waste of virtuous human resources.

"To communicate with people of inferior conduct is a waste of words.

"A wise man will not let a virtuous teacher fall into waste. Nor will he waste his words communicating with people who are weak in moral principles." (15.8)

Confucius said: "No virtuous man with a lofty ideal will beg to live at the expense of giving up the benevolent spirit.

"On the contrary, he will give up dear life in order to establish the spirit of benevolence." (15.9)

Student Gong asked about benevolence, *ren*.

Confucius said: "An artisan who sets out to do his job well will first sharpen his tools. When you settle in a new country, seek to pay respect to those who are wise and virtuous, and be friendly to those who are benevolent." (15.10)

Confucius said: "A man who is not guided by a long-term goal will be troubled by many short-term difficulties." (15.12)

Confucius said: "A man will be spared of complaints if he is critical of himself and lenient in judging others." (15.15)

Confucius said: "I cannot do much to teach those who always asked 'what to do, what to do', and seldom contemplate what they should be doing." (15.16)

Confucius said: "It would be difficult to teach virtue to those who spend their days exchanging wise cracks and are complacent on not knowing righteousness." (15.17)

Confucius said: "A gentleman judges everything relative to righteousness, and conducts himself in propriety. He is humble and sincere in his manners, and he completes his tasks to reach excellence." (15.18)

Confucius said: "A gentleman is concerned about his own inadequacies, and not about his not being recognized by others." (15.19)

Confucius said: "A gentleman is concerned that he may go

through life with no achievement to earn himself a good name." (15.20)

Confucius said: "A gentleman seeks to earn his own marks.
  "A base man seeks praise from other people." (15.21)

Confucius said: "A gentleman is prudent and free of content.
  "He is sociable but not gregarious." (15.22)

Confucius said: "A gentleman would not promote a person because of his pleasing words, nor would he dismiss a person because his words are unpleasant." (15.23)

Student Gong asked: "Is there a sentence which could guide me throughout life?"
  Confucius said: "Yes, only the word *shu*, forbearance. Do not do to others what you would not wish them to do to you." (15.24)

Confucius said: "Specious words confound virtue. Lack of patience in small issues will break down the effective completion of big plans." (15.27)

Confucius said: "We should detect why a person is hated by

people around him. Likewise, we must appreciate the reason when a person is liked by everyone." (15.28)

Confucius said: "Man is responsible for enhancing *dao*, the way of life, rather than for *dao* to enhance him." (15.29)

Confucius said: "A person who will not correct his faults is indeed a person at fault." (15.30)

Confucius said: "I have engaged myself in contemplation day and night, abstaining from food and sleep. Little was gained. It is more productive to engage in critical studies." (15.31)

Confucius said: "A gentleman could be trusted with extensive responsibilities without being examined on small matters.

"A base man should not be trusted to take big responsibilities except to be guided to improve on small matters." (15.34)

Confucius said: "When approaching benevolence, *ren*, one must not yield even to one's teacher." (15.36)

Confucius said: "A gentleman holds firm to the major principles of his belief, not its minor details." (15.37)

Confucius said: "Teach all pupils regardless of differences in their personal background. Everyone will change with education." (15.39)

Confucius said: "People with different views of life should not plot their affairs together." (15.40)

Confucius said: "With the use of language, it is most important to select and organize words to convey meaning." (15.41)

A blind musician came to visit Confucius.

When the former arrived at the stairs, Confucius said: "The stairs are in front of you." When he was ready to sit down, Confucius said: "The mat is in front of you." When everyone in the room had sat down, Confucius informed his blind friend who was sitting where in the room.

After the departure of the visitor, student Zhang asked: "Master, is what you have said just now in accordance with the rules of propriety?"

Confucius replied: "They were certainly in accord with the rules of assisting a blind friend." (15.42)

Confucius said: "There are three types of friends that can enhance your life, and three that will ruin your life.

"The first three are friends who are upright, accommodating, and well-informed.

"The second three are friends who are two-faced, obsequious, and shallow." (16.4)

Confucius said: "There are three likes that will enhance your life, and three that will ruin your life.

"Your life will be enhanced if you like to use music and the rites sparingly, to spread the good deeds of others, and to make friends with people who are virtuous and able.

"Your life will be ruined if you like to pursue extravagant pleasure, to lose yourself in aimless loitering, and to indulge in lavish feasting." (16.5)

Confucius said: "A gentleman should be vigilant against three issues, namely:

- To be vigilant against lust and sex in his youth, when physical and psychological maturity is not reached.
- To be vigilant against conflicts and fights in adulthood, when his body is strong and his energy abundant.
- To be vigilant against avarice when everything seems to be on the decline." (16.7)

Confucius said: "A gentleman should heed and respect three things. They are the givens of Heaven, the experience and wisdom of great men, and the words of sages.

"The base man does not heed nor respect the givens of Heaven because he has little knowledge about them. He heeds or respects neither the wisdom of great men nor the words of the sages because he is ignorant of them." (16.8)

Confucius said: "Those who are born to know are high in intelligence and achievement. Next in position are those who acquire knowledge through learning. Still next are those who learn because they need to solve practical problems in life. The lowest group are

people who do not learn even when confronted with difficulties."
(16.9)

Confucius said: "A gentleman should keep in his mind nine
concerns as he acts:

- He should be concerned whether he understands what he
  sees as he makes observations.
- He should be concerned whether he hears clearly as he
  listens.
- He should be concerned with detecting emotional
  meaning as he watches people's facial expressions.
- He should be concerned with discerning respect or a lack
  of it as he examines people's demeanor.
- He should be concerned with noticing the emotional
  content of speeches.
- He should be concerned with noticing the attitudes of
  workers as they discharge their responsibilities.
- He should be concerned with his own doubts so he can
  enquire about them as they arise.
- He should be concerned with his own anger and be
  aware of possible consequences.
- He should be concerned with the principles of
  righteousness and honesty when he is offered gains."
  (16.10)

Confucius said: "There are people who strive to do good ahead of
other people, and who avoid evil as abruptly as they withdraw a
hand from boiling water. I have met such men and heard such
claims.

"There are people who resort to living in seclusion in
order to achieve virtuous ideals, and who are so committed to
the righteous values that they persisted in practicing them

throughout life. I have heard people making such claims, but not encountered anyone who has carried them out." (16.11)

Chen Kang asked Confucius' son Boyu about his education at home.

Boyu said: "Once, my father was standing in the courtyard. When he saw me attempting to hastily pass by, he asked me if I had studied the *Book of Poetry*.

"I said: Not yet.

"He then said: 'You will not communicate well if you do not know this book well.'

"I retreated to study it immediately as he had advised.

"On another day, my father was standing on the same spot as I was dashing past. He stopped me again and asked if I had learned the principles of propriety.

"I said: Not yet.

"Then, he said: 'You will not be able to establish yourself as an effective person if you do not know such principles.'

"Again, I retreated to learn the principles of propriety."

Chen Kang was elated on learning about these two episodes. He murmured: "I asked one question and got three pieces of valuable information; about poetry and propriety, and about how Confucius was aloof even to his own son. It seemed that he was teaching his own son in the same way he was teaching us." (16.13)

Confucius said: "Human nature is the same in everyone.

"People became different as they grew up, being influenced and shaped by the customs and values of the community they lived in." (17.2)

Confucius said: "The two groups of people who are not easily changed are the highly gifted and the poorly endowed." (17.3)

One day, as Confucius and his students arrived at the small town of Wu Cheng, they heard an exquisite performance of chants of rites, accompanied by the playing of strings. Confucius said with a grin: "There is no need to use a butcher knife to kill a chicken."

Student You commented on observing his teacher's behavior: "Master, I heard you once said, a gentleman shows his love for the people by studying music and propriety rites, while ordinary citizens will be more pliable after they have become familiar with the same.... There is certainly merit for the leaders of Wu Cheng to emphasize the performance of music and rites."

Confucius conceded, making it known to all students present by saying: "Your words are certainly true. I was joking when I referred to the use of a butcher knife to kill a chicken." (17.4)

Student Zhang asked about benevolence, *ren*.

Confucius said: "To promote the five virtues bound by Heaven and earth is to practice *ren*."

Zhang asked for more explanation.

"Respect, generosity, trustworthiness, earnestness, and kindness are the five virtues," he continued to explain, "A person who respects others will not fall into disgrace; a person who is generous will earn the love of everyone; a person who is trustworthy will be charged with important responsibilities; a person who is earnest will achieve success; a person who is kind will gain general support in all his endeavors." (17.6)

Confucius asked student You if he had heard about the six virtuous qualities and their six associated faults. When the latter answered negatively, he said: "Sit tight and listen.

"He who practices benevolence without associating it with learning will end up being naïve.

"He who is keen to develop wisdom without a love for learning will end up in mental dissipation.

"He who loves to trust without a pursuit for learning will invite recklessness and personal danger.

"He who is forward and upright without loving to learn will be rude.

"He who is bold and does not learn will tend to be insubordinate.

"He who has a strong will without a love for learning will be unruly." (17.8)

One day, Confucius came to class and complained: "Students, why do you not study the *Book of Poetry* seriously?" as he continued to propound his views:

"Poetry awakes the imagination.

"Poetry inspires observation.

"Poetry nurtures a sense of sociability.

"Poetry facilitates the expression of feelings.

"Through your studies of poetry you can learn how to serve your parents as well as your country. Moreover, your reading will enable you to know the names of birds, animals, and trees and vegetables in nature." (17.9)

Confucius said: "When they say propriety and rites, it does not only mean the offering of jade vessels and silk strips. And when they say music, it does not mean the mere striking of bells and the beating of drums." (17.11)

Confucius said: "In promoting the essence of virtue, one does not simply repeat the gossips heard while walking on the road. To do so is to cast away the profound wisdom inherent in virtue." (17.14)

Confucius said: "The attitudes and behaviors of people in old days are quite different compared to those of people today.

"People of a bygone era who had attained noble goals were carefree in life, while people of today with similar attainments are dissolute and discourteous.

"While ancient men of dignity exhibited unreserved modesty, men in similar stance today tend to be aggressive and perverse.

"While the average person in ancient times was upright in character, the average person today is self-centered and deceitful." (17.16)

Confucius said: "What a pity that the traditional courtly vermillion is not overshadowed by the popular purple color.

"What a pity that the sweet melodies of classical music is now overpowered by the rumblings of the Zheng rhythms.

"In the same vein, how detestable it is to see people with witty persuasion succeeding in subverting our government." (17.18)

Confucius declared one day that he would refrain from speaking henceforth.

Student Gong asked: "In that case, what could we record for the benefits of future generations?"

Confucius responded: "Does Heaven speak? The four

seasons follow their natural course, hundreds of living things continue to thrive and multiply, and Heaven need not speak." (17.19)

Confucius said: "He who is content to eat and survive while doing nothing else is difficult to teach. Even he who passes his time playing chess is a better student." (17.22)

Student Gong asked his teacher: "Does a gentleman occasionally dislike others?"

Confucius replied: "Yes, he dislikes people who tell tales about others; people who, being in subordinate positions, slander their superiors; people who are quick to act giving no attention to propriety; as well as people who are willful and obstinate."

Then, he asked Gong if he had any dislikes.

Gong replied: "I detest those who violate the intellectual properties of innovators, those who cover their valor with false modesty, and those who believe it is right to expose other people's secrets." (17.24)

Confucius once confessed: "I find it difficult to interact with women and base men.

"They would recede from their normal modesty if you approached them with affection. And they would show their discontent if you stayed distant." (17.25)

Confucius said: "There is not much to be said about a man who, at forty, is still suffering from scorn and antipathy." (17.26)

Student Xia said: "Although a gentleman is not interested in learning small crafts, each and every one of them has its intriguing aspects. When observed carefully, they could reveal important knowledge." (19.4)

Student Xia said: "I might indeed be a master of my own learning if I could learn something new every day, and remembered all that I had learned when I reviewed them at the end of the month." (19.5)

Student Xia said: "There is no need to look for benevolence, *ren*. It is nested in the process of broadening one's knowledge persistently, and in making enquiries in earnest, followed by careful deliberations." (19.6)

Student Xia said: "A gentleman impresses people in three ways.

"He appears stern from a distance. He is benign in their presence. He is firm and convincing when he speaks." (19.9)

Student You once said this to his classmate Xia: "Your students are capable of taking care of daily routines. But they have yet to learn about propriety and the rites. Something must be done."

Xia retorted: "Those are frivolous and distorted observations indeed. Who has the authority to decide the sequence of learning in a gentleman's education? A gentleman's way of life is shaped by various kinds of knowledge and skills, some of which mundane, others enlightening, still others practical and empowering. Only a superior teacher, like a sage, knows exactly what to teach first and what next." (19.12)

Student Xia said: "One should continue to learn even when one performs well in one's job.

"One is appointed to high office on account of one's excellence in scholarship." (19.13)

Student Gong said: "A gentleman's mistakes are like eclipses of the sun and the moon. When they appear, everyone sees them. After they are gone, people admire the afterglow." (19.21)

Gongsun of the State of Wei asked student Gong about Confucius' mentor.

Gong replied: "The traditional wisdom of Emperors Wen and Wu are still around us. The wise and capable are tuned to its essence. The common folks are mindful of its details. Everyone knows the way of life precipitated by the great emperors. How could my teacher not learn from this great tradition. Why would he need a mentor in particular?" (19.22)

Once, the scholar Chen asked Gong: "Forget being respectful. Do you really think your teacher Confucius is better than you?"

Gong said: "We should be careful when talking about the Master. He is unreachable just as Heaven cannot be reached with a ladder.

"He teaches people to be morally good, and they abide by his rules.

"He teaches people to live peacefully and harmoniously, and they flock to his presence.

"He is greatly honored in life. He will be sorrowfully mourned in death.

"Thus, he is out of everyone's reach." (19.25)

Confucius said: "A man is not a gentleman if he does not understand the givens of life. A man is not established if he does not know propriety and the rites. A man is not in a position to know other people if he does not understand their words." (20.3)

Mencius

Introduction

Mencius was written by the scholar Mencius, together with his students Wan Zhang and Gongsun Chou, to record their views on philosophy, ethics, politics, psychology, and education. Living between 372–289 B.C., Mencius was four generations removed from Confucius. However, he was so successful in broadening and amplifying the concept of *ren*, benevolence, that a new name, "The Benevolent Way of Confucius and Mencius," was given to represent it in later history. His book was also included in the *Four Books*, a compulsory text for classical Chinese education.

Mencius the man had a unique and interesting life. His reputation as an educator and sage was shared by his mother, who had raised and educated him as a single parent. Legend has it that she moved house three times in order to avoid unwanted community influence on her young son. Once, when Mencius told her that he did not like to go to school anymore, she abruptly used a pair of scissors to sever the weaving in her loom to impress upon the child that stopping one's education half-way is like destroying the entire pattern of learning in one's life. Since weaving was the family's main source of income, young Mencius was so shocked that he vowed to dedicate his whole life to learning.

Mencius believed that human nature is good, because we were born to show compassion, to know shame and evil, to concede with our attitudes and words, and to know right and wrong. He called these "the four cardinal points of human nature." Together, they are capable of exercising "the four virtues" of *ren, yi, li, zhi*, or benevolence, righteousness, propriety, and wisdom respectively.

Mencius emphasized the use of conscience and conscientious skills which are innate to all human beings. He believed in the influences of education and environmental forces in shaping the human personality and character. He proposed that our social hierarchy be built according to the conviction that the people are of primary importance, followed by livelihood, and last, the interest and wishes of the ruler. Thus, he is recognized as the father of democratic ideals in China.

On education and self-cultivation, Mencius advocated that people should follow their human nature and inborn abilities, and store in their hearts the principles of virtue, that a person should be self-reliant as he seeks to explore the world of learning. In his own words, "A person who exhausts his mind, knows his nature, and works with the natural givens in life, will reach a situation where everything in the universe is ready for his operation."

As a synthesis of these beliefs and advocacies Mencius described the Confucian gentleman as a man who will not be corrupted by wealth and fame, nor swayed by poverty and lowliness, nor subjugated by authority and brute force. This very spirit has been revered by all Chinese through the millennia, and served as the guiding light of personality development.

However, Mencius had not met with a lot of success and satisfaction in real life. The book *Mencius* contains substantial narrations about his travels to advocate "people-centered governance" (*wangdao*) and "benevolent administration" (*renzheng*). But his views were not accepted, and he held no office in any court in his life. He returned to his native Shandong in late life, and devoted his time to teaching and writing.

There were seven chapters in the original book. Four more chapters were added in later compilations. Together, they constitute one of the most important renditions of Confucian thought and traditional Chinese wisdom.

Because the book was largely written in a recording style, it contains substantial materials pertaining to people and places, as well as events that are remote and unfamiliar to modern readers.

Much of these are also insignificant to the principal views and ideals of Mencius. Therefore, I have, in this rendition, selectively used only those parts which pertain to the main theories and themes. To facilitate smooth and coherent reading, I have also added connecting statements here and there, whenever sections of the original text have been left out.

SLK

Mencius had an audience with King Xuan of the State of Chi to discuss the characteristics of a benevolent ruler. The King asked at one point: "What virtue must a king possess so that he may be called a good king?"

Mencius replied: "To protect the people and to secure an adequate livelihood for them. Once that is evident, no one could keep you from being king."

They went on to discuss the difference between being unable to do something and not wanting to do it.

Mencius said: "Serve and respect the elders in other homes just as you would your own at home; and love and teach all children just as you would your own. Then every affair in your country will go well, as if controlled in your palm."

He continued later: "We weigh things so as to know if they are light or heavy. We measure distances so as to know if objects and places lie far or near.

"In the same vein, we can detect what is in people's mind by observations and judgment. It is up to your majesty to do that....

"If your majesty would institute a system of government based on the principle of *ren*, then all able officers in the empire would wish to work for you, farmers from everywhere would wish to farm your land, merchants and traders would wish to exchange their goods in your markets, and travelers would go through your roads. At that point, people who are dissatisfied with their own governments will flock to settle in your state. When people everywhere are so inclined, nobody in the country will be able to stop such a force....

"Without a stable income, only the educated few would hold fast to their moral principles. But common people would not uphold any moral principle devoid of a stable income. Instead, they would resort to the use of devious means to make a living, even to the extent of breaking the law. When a king makes no effort to educate his people, but subjects them to punishment when they commit crimes, it is like trapping them with a wide net...

"Therefore, a wise king will do his utmost to improve the livelihood of his people, enabling them to serve their parents adequately, and to feed their wives and children. This means that, in a year of good harvest, everyone in the family will be kept healthy; and in a bad year, no one will die of hunger.

"In the end, if schools were set up to teach people of all ages to uphold the moral principles of filial piety and righteousness, no elderly person will be seen carrying heavy loads on the roads.
...

"Under these circumstances, no one in your dominion would be so unreasonable as to refuse you their allegiance." (1A.1)

Gongsun asked Mencius: "Could you tell me the difference between how you maintain an unperturbed mind and the way that Gao Zi maintains his?"

Mencius replied: "Gao Zi often said that a person should not store in mind those thoughts which are not in accord with virtue; and a person should not exercise passion to subdue those thoughts which trouble the mind. I can concede to this last statement. But I cannot accept the first statement.

"The will is a person's driving force, and therefore master of his mind. On the other hand, passion is subservient to the will. So, to maintain an unperturbed mind, one must hold firm to one's will, and keep calm one's passion."

Gongsun said he did not understand, and asked his teacher to show how his unperturbed mind is superior.

Mencius explained: "I know the words that carry the moral principles. I am also adept in nurturing an all-embracing passion, *qi*."

Gongsun pursued: "What is this all-embracing *qi*?"

Mencius replied: "It is not easy to give it a full description. This all-embracing *qi* is both encompassing and strong.

"When it is nourished by rectitude and expanded through an

unhampered course of development, its energy can fill up the space bound by Heaven and Earth. When it is synthesized with benevolence and righteousness, this energy will gather strength and momentum as its possessor improves his character by doing one righteous deed after another. On the other hand, without benevolence and righteousness as foundation, this *qi* will lose its vitality."

Gongsun then asked about knowing the words.

Mencius replied: "When a person's speech is biased, his mind is consumed by gain. When a person's speech is discourteous and extravagant, his mind has departed from virtue. When a person's speech is non-committal, his mind is clouded by trouble. You see, people usually speak from their heart." (2A.2)

Mencius said: "People cannot bear to see other human beings suffer because they are endowed with a sympathetic heart....

"When a person suddenly sees a child about to fall into a well, he will, regardless of how aloof he may be, be alarmed and filled with compassion. He will be moved to help.

"His heart was moved not because he wished to befriend the child's parents, not because he would like the approval and praise from his chums, nor because he disliked the desperate call of the endangered child.

"We may deduce from this that a person devoid of compassion is not human, a person without the feelings of shame and evil is not human, a person who has no sense of modesty and gratitude is not human, and a person who has no sense of right and wrong is not human.

"A feeling of compassion is the source of *ren*, the spirit of benevolence.

"A feeling of shame and evil is the source of *yi*, righteousness.

"A sense of modesty and gratitude is the source of *li*, propriety.

"A sense of right and wrong is the source of *zhi*, wisdom.

"Anyone who allows his life to thrive with these four sources, and who can develop them fully, will feel within him a flame ready to burn, and a spring ready to gush.

"When these feelings and emotions are fully developed in a person, he will be powerful enough to rule the four seas. When they are ignored, he will not be able to even serve his own parents." (2A.6)

Mencius said: "Are makers of arrows less benevolent than makers of armors? Makers of arrows are concerned that their arrows cannot injure or kill soldiers during combat. Makers of armors are concerned that soldiers will not be injured or killed. The same compassion goes with the witch-doctor and the coffin maker. It is clear that a man should be careful in choosing his trade.

"As Confucius had once said, a community is good when it fosters benevolence; a man is unwise if he chooses to live in a community whose values are contrary to his.

"Benevolence is the highest honor and value bestowed by Heaven. It is also man's most tranquil residence.

"A man is unwise if he, without any hindrance imposed, does not live a benevolent life.

"A man will enslave himself if he deprives himself of the benevolent spirit, acts of conscience, and other virtuous undertakings....

"A benevolent man is like the art of archery. The archer must stand a firm and good stance before he lets go of the arrow to its aim. He should not envy the winning competitor if he misses the target. Rather, he should reflect on his own action in order to detect the mistakes made. That is the only way to improve his archery." (2A.7)

Mencius said: "Being at the opportune time is less important than having a situational advantage. Having a situational advantage is less important than being in harmony with a partner." (2B.1)

King Wen of Teng asked Mencius about government.

Mencius said: "The legendary Zhou dynasty was governed with straight rules. It also introduced effective measures to facilitate livelihood and education....

"The government established various types of schools to educate the people, including the Xiang, the Xiao, and the Xu.

"Xiang schools concentrated on teaching people about filial piety and how to take care of old folks. Xiao schools concentrated on teaching about life and virtue. Xu schools taught archery and the art of fighting.... Together, these schools taught people how to live prudently, happily, and harmoniously." (3A.3)

A visitor came to discuss good government with King Wen. After a lengthy discourse, Mencius was involved. He said: "For his deep concern about his people, the ancient sage-emperor Shun appointed Xie to be in charge of education so that good ethics would prevail in his domain.

"People were taught how fathers and sons should show affection to one another; how the sovereign and his ministers should maintain righteousness between them; how husbands and wives should attend to their different functions; how the old and the young should keep proper order; and how there must be fidelity among friends.

"The great Emperor Yao once said: 'We should instigate measures not only to settle and govern our people, but also to educate them, to give them wings, and to empower them to possess themselves.'" (3A.4)

Jing Chun said to Mencius: "Don't you think Gongsun Yan and Zhang Yi are truly magnanimous gentlemen? When they threw a rage, all the princes around were afraid. And when they were tranquil, people in the empire had no reason for unrest."

Mencius said: "Is that all there is to being a magnanimous gentleman? Have you not learned from the *Book of Rites*?

"When a young man had reached the age for the capping ceremony, his father would teach him how to conduct himself in life. When a maiden is ready for marriage, her mother would teach her how to make a good home. She would accompany her to the door to send her off, telling her that she must respect and care for her husband, and never be disobedient.

"According to the canons of virtue, compliance is a woman's way of life.

"As for men, they dwell in the grand house bound by Heaven and Earth, they stand firm on guard of the right position, and they walk on the open path of the world.

"A gentleman will apply the principles of virtue for the good of the people when he assumes a leadership position. Alternatively, when he is disposed of office, he will adhere to his principles as he lives in obscurity.

"A true gentleman will not be corrupted by wealth and fame, nor swayed by destitution and lowliness, nor be subjugated by authority and brute force." (3B.2)

Mencius was once asked: "Did men of scholarship take up government office in the old days?"

He answered: "Yes, they did. The *Record* showed that Confucius was troubled and unhappy when he was out of office for merely three months. At such times, he would travel to other states to look for an appointment, carrying gifts with him...." (3B.3)

Mencius said: "Just as a compass and a square can produce circles and squares, a sage can be a perfect example of virtue....

"Confucius told us once that there were two approaches to governance, that of benevolence and that of oppression.

"An oppressive king who tyrannized his people to an unbearable extreme would be slain, and his sovereignty torn apart.

"An oppressive king who taxed his people heavily would have himself and his sovereignty thrown into danger.

"Tyrants are marked by black names of brutality. Their bad reputation would last for hundreds of generations, even if the throne was later on succeeded by virtuous offspring...." (4A.2)

Mencius said: "When your love for another person is met with reticence, you should reflect on the quality of your love. When your guidance to another person is met with repulsion, you should reflect on your wisdom. When your courtesy shown to another person is not met with reciprocal courtesy, you should reflect on the quality of your respect.

"Whenever our words and actions fail to elicit the expected response from others, we should turn to ourselves to detect any shortcomings. Actions that reflect moral principles will have a modeling effect on others, stimulating them to join in with us to behave morally.

"It is said in the *Book of Poetry*: 'To Heaven's endowment your actions resonate, abundant happiness will rest with you day after day.'" (4A.4)

Mencius said: "It is futile to advise a man who ruins his own character, just as it is counterproductive to cooperate with one who abandons his own will.

"A man who rejects the principles of propriety and righteousness ruins his own character. A person who refuses to live out the spirit of benevolence and righteousness abandons his own will.

"*Ren* is the happy habitat of man, and *yi* his right path. Alas, could anyone be so foolish as to leave vacant his happy habitat, and not follow the right path of life?" (4A.10)

Mencius said: "The right way of life is close to every human being, but people tend to seek it from afar.

"It is easy to follow the *Way* in all our pursuits, but people choose to do what is difficult.

"When everybody loves their parents and respects their elders, peace will prevail all over the world." (4A.11)

Mencius said: "A man must follow the *Way* in order to earn the trust of his friends. He will not be trusted if he does not serve his parents well.

"A man must follow the *Way* in order to please his parents. He will not please his parents if he is not sincere to everyone.

"A man must follow the *Way* in order to keep his body and mind in a sincere position. He will not attain sincerity if he fails to do good.

"It is evident that sincerity is the *Way of Heaven* (a universal way of life). To be vigilant on behaving sincerely is the *Way of man*.

"Never has there been a sincere person who could not touch another person's heart, nor is there an insincere person who could win other people's trust." (4A.12)

Mencius said: "The pupils in a man's eyes are the most revealing part of his body, they cannot conceal any wickedness in him.

"If a man's heart is kind and virtuous, his pupils will shine brightly. If his heart is devious, the pupils will appear dull and dim.

"We can therefore delineate whether a man is kind or unkind by first listening to his words, then observing his eyes. It is not possible for anyone to conceal the quality of his character." (4A.15)

Mencius said: "A humble and respectful person does not cheat. A prudent person does not exploit. A ruler who exploits his people is neither humble nor prudent; he is actually afraid that his rule is in jeopardy.

"It is not possible to falsify humility and prudence with a grand display of smiles and pleasing tones." (4A.16)

Kun from the State of Qi asked Mencius: "Is it true that propriety dictates that a man and a woman must not have any physical contact when doing a transaction?"

Mencius replied: "Yes, that is the rule in the rites."

"Should a man extend his hand to save his drowning sister-in-law?" asked Kun.

"A man is not different from an animal if he does not do so," said Mencius, "The rule of rites that forbids men and women to show their affection with physical contact is a general rule. Extending a helping hand to save your drowning sister-in-law is a case of exigency."

Kun asked again: "Today, people in our entire country are drowning from the ills of corruption, why do you not reach out to save them?"

Mencius replied: "We use moral principles to save a nation from drowning in corruption. We use a hand to pull a sister-in-law out of drowning in water. Why, do you say I should rescue a corrupting nation with my hands?" (4A.17)

Gongsun asked: "Why do gentlemen not teach their own children personally?"

Mencius replied: "It is because the situation is not conducive to its being done well. For example, a teacher must stand firm when he helps his pupil to inculcate moral principles. The expectation is that it is not enough for a pupil to know the virtues; he must also practice them. When the teacher discovers that it is not done, he is naturally upset, and his anger would antagonize the pupil.

"A father sets out to teach his child with affection. If he becomes angry like the teacher mentioned above, he would likewise antagonize his son. The son will then say: 'Father, you taught me the virtue of harmony, but you behaved in disharmony. How could I learn from you?' Then, the relationship between father and son begins to deteriorate.

"In ancient times, parents often exchanged positions in teaching their children so they could avoid confrontation and direct admonition. For they knew teaching one's own child could lead to alienation. And alienation could lead to estrangement in what should be a loving relationship." (4A.18)

Mencius said: "The most important service a man is obliged to give is service to his parents. The most important thing a man is obliged to sustain is his integrity and good character....

"To serve one's parents with adequate provisions and respect is the root of all services. To sustain one's good character with virtue is the root of all preservations...." (4A.19)

Mencius said: "A man who is seldom reproved will tend to speak with a quick tongue." (4A.20)

Mencius said: "A man's most serious weakness is his being overly ready to teach others." (4A.23)

Mencius said: "There are three faults in falling short of filial piety, the worst is to have no heir. The great Shun got married without consulting his parents, because he was anxious to maintain posterity. When scholars appraised his action in ensuing ages, they did not blame him for what he had done." (4A.26)

Mencius said: "The essence of being benevolent is to serve one's parents. The essence of being righteous is to yield to the command of one's elder brothers. The essence of being wise is to perform the above two tasks steadfastly. The essence of propriety is to coordinate the practice of benevolence and righteousness. The essence of happiness is to take pride in one's benevolent and righteous actions.

"Once a man is happy, he will be so naturally pleased that his arms and legs are free to dance without inhibition." (4A.27)

Mencius said: "Only the great Shun could have people from all over his empire submit to him readily.

"A man could hardly be called a man if he failed to serve his parents to their delight. He could not be called a son if he failed to follow his parents' aspirations.

"Shun did his best to serve his father and let him feel the

pleasure of being virtuous and good. His example transformed the whole empire, and established in it the duties of children to their parents. That was an example of good filial piety." (4A.28)

Mencius said: "It is the responsibility of the morally distinguished man to inculcate the ordinary people with moral principles. It is the obligation of the able to teach the less able. That is why people generally wished to have parents and elders who exemplify virtue and ability.

"If the virtuous and the able elite in the community did not live up to these teaching expectations, there could be no differentiation between good and bad, able and unable." (4B.7)

Mencius said: "A man must know what he would not do before he can achieve what he wills to do." (4B.8)

Mencius said: "A man who is quick to speak about another man's wrongs should be prepared to accept the consequence of impending counter-attacks by others." (4B.9)

Mencius said: "Confucius would not go to extremes when relating to people and things." (4B.10)

Mencius said: "A great man is not expected to keep his words and to account for his deeds at all times. But he is expected to always keep the principle of *yi* in his mind." (4B.11)

Mencius said: "A great man keeps alive in his personality the innocence of a newborn baby." (4B.12)

Mencius said: "A gentleman learns by the method of generic learning. Through this process knowledge will reside deep in his mind, allowing him to draw from it as if he were drawing water from a spring. This is why a gentleman learns to master the art of generic learning." (4B.14)

Mencius said: "A person who learns broadly and in accurate detail will acquire knowledge so soundly that he is able to express it in simple and meaningful terms." (4B.15)

Mencius said: "No one has been able to convince others with truth. But people could be won through education.

"I have not seen a case where a leader could earn the right to rule before he had won the heart of the people." (4B.16)

Student Xu asked: "Confucius used to praise water, saying, 'Ah, water, ah, water.' I wonder what he saw in it?"

Mencius replied: "Water that trickles from a mountain spring can run ceaselessly day and night. After it has filled all the low spots on a plain it continues to advance its course, until it has reached the ocean.

"What Confucius found so commendable about it is that all flowing water that comes from a source eventually gets to the ocean. Water that does not, such as the torrents that pour down from the sky in the summer, will be dried up one day, even if it may fill up a few brooklets on the plain.

"A scholar who enjoys a reputation beyond his merit is similar to a body of water without a source. He should feel ashamed of it because it will vanish one day." (4B.18)

Mencius said: "There is not much difference between human beings and birds and beasts ... While ordinary people ignore such differences, the gentleman pays great attention to them.

"The sage, Shun, understood many dimensions of man and his world, including the ethics among men. He practiced benevolence and righteousness as an integral part of human nature, not just as a means to an end." (4B.19)

Mencius said: "If a man is confronted with taking something or not taking something, taking it would violate the virtue of frugality. If a man is confronted with giving something or not giving it, giving it would not be showing a favor. If a man is confronted with a choice of to die or not to die, choosing to die is not necessarily an act of courage." (4B.23)

Mencius said: "It is possible to investigate the nature of things by extrapolating from past events. Regrettably, some clever individuals claim to know the nature of things based on their own presumptions.

"Though the sky is high and the stars are far away, if we made investigations on how they had appeared in the past, we could calculate the winter solstice of a millennium hence." (4B.26)

Mencius said: "The difference between a gentleman and an ordinary man is marked by what is stored in their hearts. The gentleman had ingrained in his heart the spirits of benevolence and propriety.

"A benevolent man loves people. A man of propriety respects people.

"He who loves others will be perpetually loved by them.

"He who respects others will be perpetually respected by them.

"When a gentleman is treated rudely and perversely by another man, he would surely reflect on his own behavior to see if he did treat that man unkindly or impolitely. He believes that people would not be adverse to one another under normal circumstances.

"If his self-reflection proved that he had not been on the wrong side, and the other man persisted in treating him in an adverse manner, the gentleman would reflect again to see if he had been wrong.

"If this second self-reflection revealed that he had not been unkind or impolite, but the other man went on treating him adversely, the gentleman would conclude that this other man must have lost his mind and, being in that state of mind, he was not different from birds and beasts. With that observation in mind the gentleman will have nothing to do with him.

"Thus, a gentleman has a lifelong concern that his self-reflection might never be adequate. But then, he has no need to worry that calamity might fall on him one day. Rather, his worry is that he will never measure up to the achievements of the great Shun, who was the role model for people of all times. This gives him the impetus for trying very hard to be a perfect gentleman through life...." (4B.28)

Mencius said: "There are five types of behavior commonly recognized as not being in conformity with filial piety:

- Not lifting one's hands and feet as one attends to the needs of one's parents.
- Indulging in gambling and drinking, and being distracted from attending to the needs of one's parents.
- Overemphasis on making money, and in siding with one's wife and children, thereby neglecting one's own parents.
- Indulging in the pleasures of theaters and salons, thereby shaming one's parents.
- Addicted to fights and quarrels, thereby endangering one's parents. (4B.30)

Mencius said: "A man admires his parents in his childhood. When he grows up and has sex drives, he will admire members of the opposite sex. After marriage, he will admire his wife. When he serves in public office, he will admire his superior or king. In all these, the man would feel anxiety if his admiration is not appreciated.

"The highest sign of filial piety is seen in a lifelong admiration of one's parents, as demonstrated by the great Shun. He persisted in admiring his parents after he was fifty years old." (5A.1)

Student Wan asked about friendship.

Mencius said: "Friends are made without regard to age seniority, social status, or wealth. Friendship with a person is friendship with his character and virtue, not anything else...." (5B.3)

Mencius said: "A man does not seek a government job to release himself from poverty. However, he will do so if it helps him to provide for his parents' needs.

"A man does not get married for the sake of obtaining personal service. But he will do so if his wife's service is helpful to his parents.

"When a man takes up a government post in order to rid himself of poverty, he should choose a low position over a high one, and a meager salary over a lofty one....

"When Confucius was a minor officer in charge of a warehouse, all that he had to do was to keep an accurate account of the flow of grains. At another time, when he was in charge of the livestock, his total concern was to keep the cattle fed and in good health.

"It would be an offence for a man in a low position to give a loud opinion on major government affairs. On the other hand, it is a shame for a man in high position to display immoral behavior." (5B.5)

Gao said to Mencius: "Human nature can be compared to purple willows, pliable yet unbendable. Righteousness can be compared to cups and plates. To embed benevolence and righteousness into human nature is like making cups and plates out of purple willow wood."

Mencius replied: "Do you mean that one should account for the special qualities of the wood in carving cups and plates out of purple willows? Or, do you mean to carve the cups and plates without regard for the natural qualities of the wood? If it is the latter case, then you will be violating a man's natural qualities as you inculcate in him the spirits of benevolence and righteousness. Alas! Your claims would undoubtedly lead people to regard benevolence and righteousness as contrary to human nature." (6A.1)

Gao said to Mencius: "Human nature is like a body of whirling water in a pond. Open a gap east in the pond, it will flow eastward; open a gap west in the pond, it will flow westward. Just as water is indifferent in flowing east or west, human nature is indifferent to good or evil."

Mencius replied: "It is true that water is indifferent in flowing eastward or westward, but could it be true that it is also indifferent in flowing upward or downward?

"Just as water follows its nature to flow downward, man is by nature good. There is no case that water does not flow downward, just as there is no case that human beings are not good.

"Speaking of water, you may beat water to make it leap upward, causing it to reach the height of your forehead. Or, you may move it upward by bailing and damming, moving water to reach the top of a mountain. However, these phenomena cannot be attributed to the nature of water. It was the external force applied to it that determined its movements.

"In the same vein, human beings can be made to behave against their own nature, such as to do evil. Human nature can be altered by external forces too." (6A.2)

Gao said to Mencius: "What is innate is called nature?"

Mencius replied: "Do you mean that in the same way as you said that whiteness is seen in all white things?"

"Yes," said Gao.

"You mean to say that the whiteness of a white feather is the same as that of white snow; and the same is true between white snow and white jade?"

"Yes," said Gao

"Then, you would make no distinction between the nature of dogs and cows, and between cows and human beings?" (6A.3)

Gao said: "To enjoy good food and delight in beautiful colors are aspects of human nature. The spirit of benevolence rests in one's heart, not to be seen from outside. The spirit of righteousness is seen in external behavior, and not to be judged from within."

Mencius asked: "On what basis do you make such claims?"

Gao said: "I say righteousness is external because when I see an elderly man, I honor him with respect. This respect did not dwell in my heart. It was something that I do. It is the same as I called the color white as I saw it on the surface of a thing. It is something external."

Mencius said: "I grand you that there is no difference between the whiteness of a white horse and that of a white man. But, is there no difference between your deference to an old horse and your respect for an old man? Further, do you regard righteousness as a part of old age, or as a part of your respect for an elderly person?"

Gao said: "I love my brother because he is my brother. I would not love this same man if he was a brother of a man from Qin. Because this differentiation of love comes from my heart, that is why I say benevolence is internal.

"I respect an elder from Chu, just as I revere the elder from my own country.

"That is why I consider righteousness to be an external quality."

Mencius replied: "A piece of meat roasted by a cook from Qin tastes just as delicious as one roasted by a cook at home. Would you then say that the enjoyment of a good roast is an external matter?" (6A.4)

Mencius said: "Every man carries a sense of compassion in his heart. Every man carries a sense of shame and dislike of evil in his heart. Every person has in his heart a sense of respect and reverence. Every man has in his heart a sense of accepting what is good and rejecting what is evil.

"Compassion is the basis of benevolence. Shame and a dislike of evil form the basis of righteousness. Respect and reverence for the good and the dignified constitute the foundation for propriety. Acceptance of the good and rejection of the evil constitute the foundation for wisdom.

"Benevolence, righteousness, propriety, and wisdom are not infused into the human heart from external forces and mechanisms. Rather, they are our natural endowments, although we are not always conscious of them.

"Thus, it was said that a man will have benevolence, righteousness, propriety, and wisdom if he only seeks and possesses them. Reversely, he will lose them if he neglects or fails to pursue them.

"People differ greatly with regard to their ability and their will to activate these four inborn qualities. Those who succeed can achieve twice, five times, even countless times the accomplishments of those who neglect to exercise them.

"As said in a poem in the *Book of Poetry*: 'Man is born of divine forces, all things follow their own laws. As seen through the nature of their own being, virtue is appreciated by all.'

"Confucius once said: 'The poet really understands the *Way*. He confirms that every single thing in the world has its own law. People who hold on to these constant laws will love virtue.'" (6A.6)

Mencius said: "... People are generally alike in the way they taste with their mouths, hear with their ears, and see with their eyes. With regard to the mind, do minds alone have no commonalities?

"In what manner would people's minds strike a common cord? It is in the way they understand the laws of nature and the orderly functioning of all things.

"Our sages knew the commonality of the human mind. I am accordingly pleased that I share this same view. Just as I enjoy the taste of meat in general, I also find pleasure in abiding by the natural law and the righteous spirit." (6A.7)

Mencius said: "... Could it be true that some people do not have the spirit of benevolence and righteousness dwelling in their hearts?

"The answer is that they might exhibit a lack of these spirits, just like mountains appear barren because trees have been cut down from them, and replenishment has not been made.

"People who appeared to have lost their spirit of benevolence and righteousness might reflect on their behavior at moments of tranquility, and regain their natural good hearts from time to time. But their daily activities are such that they lose touch with their good conscience again and again. At that point, they are no different from wild beasts.

"People may hastily conclude that, because some people exhibit evil behavior, human nature is bad. But the goodness of human nature is defined by the existence of benevolence and righteousness rather than behavior.

"If, on the other hand, the people who had exhibited evil behavior were given appropriate education and socialization, they would surely regain in their hearts the natural spirits of benevolence and righteousness that were there....

"Confucius once said: 'Exercise your spirits of virtue and they will remain; abandon them, they will perish. For such spirits appear and disappear in no definite time, nor do we know where in our hearts they rest.' I believe Confucius was referring to the human mind." (6A.8)

Mencius said: "... Take the case of learning to play chess. Although it is a small art, its top skills cannot be mastered if a man is not committed to learn.

"If the best player in our country was to teach two beginners to play chess, the one who was determined to learn would certainly succeed. But the other, while he appeared to be listening to the teacher, his mind was occupied by the expected appearance of a beautiful swan and its impending capture by him. He would definitely not succeed with his learning.

"Could it be that the second student had an inferior intelligence compared to his successful classmate? I would say not." (6A.9)

Mencius said: "I delight in eating fish the same as I enjoy eating bear paws. However, if I cannot have both, I will take the bear paw.

"To be alive is important to me, just as to be righteous. However, if I cannot keep the two together, I would rather be righteous than alive at all cost....

"Life is very precious to me. But there is something more precious than life. It is therefore natural that I will not keep myself alive under all conditions.

"Death is what I detest. But there is something that I detest more. I therefore will not save myself from death at all cost....

"Everyone knows that there are things or situations more precious than life, and there are things and situations worse than death. That is why the virtuous man chooses to die in order to preserve what is larger than life. He will also choose to avoid danger in order to achieve what is constructive. The only difference between a virtuous man and people in general is that the former makes such righteous choice consistently throughout his life...." (6A.10)

Mencius said: "Benevolence is a person's heart, and righteous his path. Alas! Shame on those who choose not to follow the path.

Also, shame on those who have lost their virtuous hearts, and make no attempt to retrieve them.

"People are quick to retrieve their chicks and dogs which have gone astray. But they are reluctant to regain the lost conscience in their hearts." (6A.11)

Gongdu asked: "Since all human beings are the same, why do some become great men while others remain lowly?"

Mencius replied: "Those who steadily pursue the great objectives consonant with human nature are great. Those who busy themselves with satisfying their sensual pleasures remain lowly."

Gongdu asked further: "Why do some people pursue their great objectives and others get busy in satisfying their sensual desires?"

Mencius said: "Ears and eyes are sensory organs that do not think, their intakes can easily be blocked by external factors. When things in our environment interact with one another, their actions could attract the attention of the ears and eyes, leading people's hearing and sight to respond at random.

"On the one hand, the mind is an organ for thought. It is endowed with the ability to think and to achieve. Once a man has recognized the unlimited capabilities of his mental functions, no amount of mundane activity will distract him from achieving greatness. On the other hand, those who fail to recognize their own mental potentials will tend to be idle, and resort to pleasing their senses." (6A.15)

Mencius said: "Honor of Heaven and honor among men exist side by side. The first type of honor is conferred to people who practice benevolence, righteousness, loyalty, and trustfulness, who, at the same time, also delight in doing good and helping the needy.

"The second type of honor is conferred to people who are dukes and high-ranking officers.

"People in bygone days strove to obtain honor of Heaven by learning to be virtuous and doing good. They used to obtain both kinds of honor by so doing.

"People today strive to obtain honor of Heaven in order to obtain official titles. They will abandon learning and good deeds the minute they have the honors among men. This is a foolish approach because, by so doing, these people could easily lose both types of honor." (6A.16)

Mencius said: "Benevolence can overcome ruthlessness, just as water can extinguish fire.

"Nowadays, there are individuals who, claiming to practice benevolence, behave in such a way as though they could put out fire from a cartload of burning wood with a cup of water. Then, when they do not succeed, they conclude that water cannot extinguish fire and, by extension, benevolence cannot overcome ruthlessness.

"Such individuals would then join the ruthless people to denounce the merit of benevolence altogether. In the end, people would believe that benevolence is a useless quality, and allow ruthlessness to reign." (6A.18)

Mencius said: "The seeds of the five kinds of grains are the best to sprout and grow. Yet, they are no more useful than the seeds of weeds, if they were not allowed to ripen.

"It is the same with the spirit of benevolence. Its potentials cannot actualize fully in a man, unless he is allowed to mature gradually." (6A.19)

Mencius said: "The great archer Yi taught archery by showing his students how to draw the bow fully before letting the arrow go. His students followed suit and became good archers.

"When the finest carpenter taught his craft, he showed his apprentice how to apply the compass and the square. The latter learned to measure and gauge with great precision." (6A.20)

Mencius said: "... Thus, before the heavenly authority entrusts a man with an extensive mission, it would first labor his mind and will, exhaust his muscles and joints, subject his body through hunger, deplete his possessions, and confound his every action. Such measures will reinforce his motivation, temper his emotions, and empower him to accomplish what seemed impossible.

"A man who makes mistakes often will learn to correct himself. A man who is perplexed will learn to solve problems and create. When he has reached full understanding, he will wear a confident smile to communicate his total mastery with words bursting from his mouth....

"We may conclude that affliction and anguish enable a man to thrive, while complacency and pleasure lead him to collapse and obliteration." (6B.15)

Mencius said: "There are many ways to teach effectively. When I refuse to teach a man, I am actually teaching him something." (6B.16)

Mencius said: "A man who constantly works his mind to its fullest extent will know himself well. He will know his life with all its endowments.

"A man who keeps his mind working to develop its finest qualities will be able to live in concert with what is given to him by Nature.

"When a man is unconcerned about the length of his life, and does his best in developing his mind and body, he will gain independence in charting and establishing his own destiny." (7A.1)

Mencius said: "Everything in life has its natural course. A man who understands all the natural courses will conduct his life smoothly and successfully; he will, for example, never stand next to a precipitous wall.

"A man who spends his life following the natural courses will die an appointed and peaceful death. On the other hand, one whose life is full of irregularities and evil deeds will die an unexpected and difficult death." (7A.2)

Mencius said: "The process of seeking to know truth is more important than getting the truth, because a seeking person is a knower.

"On the other hand, if one seeks truth without understanding it, then, even when the truth is present, it lies outside the seeker." (7A.3)

Mencius said: "The true courses of everything are already resting in my heart. How delightful it would be that, by repeated self-reflection, I discovered my own genuineness. All that remains for me to do is to persist in treating others in ways that I would wish to be treated by them. I would then know that I am not far from approaching benevolence." (7A.4)

Mencius said: "Too many people do things without knowing why. Their actions become routine and habitual, with no reflective observation to find out their purpose or consequence. In this way they act mechanically and unknowingly." (7A.5)

Mencius said: "No one could be without a sense of shame. Not knowing shame is shameful to the utmost degree." (7A.6)

Mencius said: "Having a sense of shame is of great importance in life. People who are cunning and crafty bear no sense of shame. In that stance they have nothing to compare with everybody else as man." (7A.7)

Mencius said: "... Devoid of office a gentleman will hold to himself, perfecting his thoughts and actions. Once appointed to office, he will behave virtuously and help everyone to do the same." (7A.9)

Mencius said: "Keep people working hard to enrich their lives, no one will complain. Carry out fair and just executions in order to maintain social order, even the man to be executed would not murmur." (7A.12)

Mencius said: "Benevolent words do not touch people as much as benevolent deeds. Effective laws do not inspire followers as much as education.

"People treat effective laws with apprehension. They participate in education with respect and expectation.

"Laws are instrumental in collecting taxes, while education helps to win people's hearts." (7A.14)

Mencius said: "The ability a person has without learning is inborn ability. The knowledge a person has without learning is innate knowledge.

"All infants love their parents naturally. They will love their elder brothers and sisters as they grow older. Love for parents is benevolence. Respect for elder siblings is righteousness. These are universal virtues." (7A.15)

Mencius said: "It is simple to be a good person. Do not be involved in actions which are against righteousness, or in desires which are contrary to righteousness." (7A.17)

Mencius said: "People develop virtue, wisdom, ability, and understanding under adverse conditions. No wonder those estranged ministers and sons of concubines, who live in a state of constant apprehension and crisis, can reach heights in these areas." (7A.18)

Mencius said: "There are people who serve heads of states to curry favor from them. There are people who serve the community to ensure security and prosperity for everyone.

"There are people who strive to learn and develop moral principles that echo the call of Heaven. They would test use these principles among people, and apply them for the benefit of the country.

"There are scholars who strive to improve themselves continually to grasp what is good and true. They will then teach the people how to do the same." (7A.19)

Mencius said: "The gentleman finds gratification in three areas, and to be head of state is not among them.

"The first gratification is that his parents and siblings are all alive and well.

"The second gratification is to have no regrets in answering to Heaven and, among people on Earth, he has done nothing to be ashamed of.

"The third gratification is that he is in the company of talented people to share all that he knows...." (7A.20)

Mencius said: "... The gentleman has harbored deep in his heart benevolence, righteousness, propriety, and wisdom.

"These natural qualities are manifest in his looks and reflected in the movements of his body. He need not speak, yet people are convinced of his fine nature." (7A.21)

Mencius said: "... The nature of water is such that it will not advance before it had filled the low lands along its course. And so it is with the nature of the gentleman who is committed to embracing the spirits of benevolence and righteousness. He will not rest until he has acquired full understanding and followed the practice of the sages." (7A.24)

Mencius said: "Everything that Yang Zi has obtained is for himself. He will not pluck a single hair from himself, even if it could benefit all his countrymen.

"Mo Zi practices universal love. You could search him from head to heel, and be convinced that he would do anything to enhance the wellbeing of people in his country.

"Zi Mo takes the middle course between Yang Zi and Mo Zi. On the surface, it looks as if he is nearer to the *Way*. But, because he holds firm to his belief with no flexibility, he is holding an exclusive view tinted by bias.

"By insisting on a single point of view, he has actually excluded a hundred other possible views." (7A.26)

Mencius said: "To serve food to a man without love is like treating him as a pig. To love a man without respect is no different from loving a pet. Respect dwells in one's heart before material provisions. A gentleman would not be retained by a gift unaccompanied by a show of respect." (7A.37)

Mencius said: "A gentleman conducts his teaching in five different ways:

- For the student who is approaching understanding, he facilitates his learning in such a way as Nature provides a timely shower to flowers ready to bloom.
- For the student set on learning the principles of virtue, he demonstrates his virtuous behaviors in all circumstances.
- For the student who excels in intelligence, he helps to develop all his talents.
- For the discerning student, he provides lots of opportunities for questions and answers.

- For the student who quietly perfects himself, he offers personal guidance and encouragement." (7A.40)

Student Gongsun asked: "Moral principles are lofty and admirable. Learning them, however, is like climbing stairs to ascend to Heaven, difficult and counterproductive. Why do we not lower the standards so that people will happily learn and habitually practice?"

Mencius said: "... A gentleman will teach his students in a way similar to how Yi taught archery. He drew his bow fully without discharging the arrow, just to show his eagerness to shoot. He also explained his correct poise in relation to his aim. When the teacher adopts a neutral position in demonstrating his process, the student will see his way clearly. He will be eager to follow it." (7A.41)

Mencius said. "A man who aborts his action when he should not do so will terminate any action he takes. A man who should enhance another man but abuses him instead will abuse anyone he encounters. A man who advances ruthlessly will fall back quickly in his course." (7A.44)

Mencius said: "A gentleman cares for all things and creatures without having to show benevolence. He treats all people with benevolence without necessarily showing affection. He is affectionate to his kin, benevolent to other people, and caring for all things." (7A.45)

Mencius said: "I know from now on the serious consequence of killing someone's close kin. When you kill a man's father or brother, he will surely reciprocate by killing your father or brother. In this way, although no one could say that you have killed your own dear ones, you have, in fact, virtually done so." (7B.7)

Mencius said: "A man who does not behave benevolently and righteously cannot expect his wife and children to do so.

"A man who does not lead other people in a benevolent and righteous way cannot expect his wife and children to follow him." (7B.9)

Mencius said: "A man who is sufficiently rich will not die of starvation even in a year of famine. A man who is full of virtue will not be lured to corruption in times of social turbulence." (7B.10)

Mencius said: "In any country, the people are of primary importance, followed by tradition and the general wellbeing of communities. The ruler or king is third and last in importance." (7B.14)

Mencius said: "To be benevolent is human. The union between people and benevolence is the *Way*." (7B.16)

Mencius said: "... A person liked by others is good. A person whose goodness shines from the heart is genuine. A person who shines with perfect virtue is beautiful. A person whose shining character enlightens people is great.

"When a great man exerts his influence to transform others, he is a sage. When a sage is perfect to the point of intrigue, he is a spiritual force for all people." (7B.25)

According to Mencius, "All human beings have things they could not bear to experience. One becomes a benevolent man when he can bear aversions.

"All human beings have things they do not wish to do. One becomes a righteous man when he is willing to confront adversity.

"When all people have in their hearts a dislike of hurting others, benevolence prevails.

"When all people have in their hearts a dislike of cheating and stealing, righteousness prevails.

"A man who is so confident about his own virtue that he is unaffected by disdain or contempt will act righteously wherever he goes...." (7B.31)

Mencius said: "Good expressions are those which use simple words to denote complex meanings. Simple operations which carry principles of virtue to impact on all situations are good actions.

"A gentleman demonstrates virtuous principles in all his daily sayings. His behaviors, while reflecting his personal purification, have a power to keep the world in peace and harmony.

"The ill with some people is that they leave their own fields unplowed, while they sow weeds in other people's fields. They criticize other people severely while remaining lenient with their own bad conduct." (7B.32)

Mencius said: "The best way to cultivate a good heart is to minimize desires.

"A man with few desires will have abundant opportunities to practice benevolence and righteousness.

"On the other hand, a man with many desires will have little room in his heart for benevolence and righteousness." (7B.35)

Glossary

Ai 哀 (Duke)
Bai Gui 白圭
bi zhong 筆塚
Boyu 伯魚
Cai 蔡 (state)
Chai 柴
Chan 禪
Chen Kang 陳亢
Chen 陳 (scholar)
Chen 陳 (state)
Cheng 程
Cheng 根 (student)
Chi 赤 (student)
chi 恥
Chi 齊
Ci 賜
Congxi 公西
Dacheng Zhixing
  Wenxuanwang 大成至聖文
  宣王
Damo 達摩
dao 道
Daxue 大學
Fan 樊 (student)
Gao Zi 告子
Gao 羔 (student)
Gaoyao 皋陶
Gongye Chang 公冶長

Gong 貢 (student)
Gongdu 公都
Gongsun Chou 公孫丑
Gongsun Yan 公孫衍
Guan Ju 關雎
Han 漢
Hui 回 (= Yan Hui 顏回,
  student)
Ji Kang 季康 (friend)
Ji Wen 季文 (scholar)
Ji 季 (student)
Jin 荊 (Duke)
Jing Chun 景春
junzi 君子
Kang 康
Kong Wen Tze 孔文子
Kuang 匡
Kun 髡
Lei 誄
Li ji 禮記
li 里
li 禮
lian 廉
Lin 林 (student)
Lu 路 (student)
Lunyu 論語
Meng 孟 (student)
Mengzi 孟子

Min 閔 (student)

Mo Zi 墨子

Nan Rong 南容

Peng 彭 (scholar)

qi 氣

Qi 齊

Qi 齊 (state)

Qin Shihuang 秦始皇

Qin 秦

Qiu 求 (student)

Qu fu 曲阜

Ran 冉 (student)

ren 仁

renzheng 仁政

Shang 商

Shangdong 山東

Shao 韶

Shi jing 詩經

Shi 師

Shun 舜 (Emperor)

Si Ma 司馬

Si shu 四書

Song 宋

Tang 唐

Tang 湯 (Emperor)

Teng 滕

Wan Zhang 萬章

Wan 萬 (student of Mencius)

wangdao 王道

Wei 衛 (Duke)

Wei 衛 (state)

Wen 文 (Emperor)

Wu Cheng 武城

Wu Daozi 吳道子

Wu 武 (Emperor)

Xia 夏 (student)

Xiang 庠

Xiao 校

Xie 契

Xu 序

Xu 徐 (student of Mencius)

Xuan 宣

Ya 雅

Yan 晏 (scholar)

Yang Zi 楊子

Yao 堯

Ye 葉 (Duke)

Yi jing 易經

Yi 沂 (river)

Yi 羿 (archer)

yi 義

Yiyin 伊尹

Yong 庸

You 有/游 (students)

Yuan Rang 原壤 (friend)

yue 樂

Zai 宰 (student)

Zeng Zi 曾子 (student)

Zhang Yi 張儀

Zhang 張 (student)

Zheng 鄭

zhi 智

Zhi 摯

Zhong yong 中庸

Zhong 中

Zhong 仲 (student)

Zhou 周 (Duke)

Zhu Xi 朱熹

Zhu Zi 朱子

Zi Mo 子莫

Zi Si 子思

Zong 頌